Yea, Hath God Said?

Yea, Hath God Said?

The Framework Hypothesis /
Six-Day Creation Debate

Kenneth L. Gentry, Jr., Th.M., Th.D.
Michael R. Butler, M.A.

Wipf and Stock Publishers

199 West 8th Avenue • Eugene OR 97401

Yea, Hath God Said?:

The framework hypothesis/six day creation debate

© 2002 Gentry Family Trust, udt April 2, 1999 and Michael R. Butler

ISBN:-159244-016-9

Professors Gentry and Butler serve on the faculty of Westminster Classical College and may be contacted at WCC's Administrative Office, 14 Woodbine Circle, Elkton, Maryland 21921 or by e-mail through www.westminsterclassicalcollege.org

For additional educational materials by Dr. Gentry, see his website:

Wipf and Stock Publishers
199 West 8th Ave., Suite 3
Eugene OR 97401

CONTENTS

Part IV. Concluding Remarks

ABBREVIATIONS

Allis   Allis, O. T. *God Spake By Moses*. Nutley, N.J.: Presbyterian and Reformed, 1951.

Berkhof   Berkhof. Louis. *Systematic Theology.* Grand Rapids: Eerdmans, 1941.

Blocher   Blocher, Henri, *In the Beginning: The Opening Chapters of Genesis.* Downers Grove, Ill.: InterVarsity, 1984.

Cassuto   Cassuto, Umberto. *A Commentary on the Book of Genesis: Part I: From Adam to Noah,* trans. Israel Abrahams. Jerusalem: Magnes, 1961.

Dabney   Dabney, Robert L. *Lectures in Systematic Theology.* Grand Rapids: Zondervan, rep.1973 [1878]).

Futato   Futato, Mark. "Because It Had Rained: A Study of Gen 2:5-7 With Implications for Gen 2:4-25 and Gen 1:1-2:3. *Westminster Theological Journal* 60:1 (Spring, 1998): 1-21.

Hall   Hall, David W. "What Was the View of the Westminster Divines on Creation Days?" In Pipa (q.v.)

Harris   Harris, R. Laird. "The Length of Creative Days in Genesis 1." In Pipa (q.v.).

Hamilton   Victor R. Hamilton, *The Book of Genesis: Chapters 1-17.* Grand Rapids: Eerdmans, 1990.

Irons   Irons, Charles Lee. "The Framework Interpretation: Explained and Defended." By author. (February 4, 1998).

Irons, "Divines"   Irons. "In the Space of Six Days: What Did the Divines Mean?," an internal Committee discussion paper, "The Report of the Committee to Study the Framework Hypothesis," Majority Report. Presbytery of Southern California (OPC). October 15-16, 1999.

Keil and Delitzsch Keil, C. F., and Delitzsch, F. *Commentary on the Old Testament*, vol. 1: *The Pentateuch,* trans. by James Martin. Grand Rapids: Eerdmans, rep. 1975.

Kelly   Kelly, Douglas F. *Creation and Change.* Ross-shire, Great Britain: Mentor, 1997.

Kidner	Kidner, Derek. *Genesis: An Introduction and Commentary.* Downers' Grove, Ill.: Inter-Varsity Press, 1967.
Kidner, "Wet or Dry?"	Kidner. "Genesis 2:5-6: Wet Or Dry?" *Tyndale Bulletin.* 17 (1966): 109-14.
Kline, "Genesis"	Kline, Meredith G. "Genesis" in Donald Guthrie and J. A. Motyer, eds., *The Eerdmans Bible Commentary.* 3d. ed.: Grand Rapids: Eerdmans, 1970.
Kline, "Glory"	Kline. "Creation in the Image of the Glory-Spirit." *Westminster Theological Journal,* 39 (1977) 250-272.
Kline, "Rain"	Kline. "Because It Had Not Rained." *Westminster Theological Journal.* 20 (May, 1958): 146-57.
Kline, "Space and Time"	Kline. "Space and Time in the Genesis Cosmogony." *Perspectives on Science and Christian Faith.* 48:1 (March 1996): 2-15.
Majority Report	"The Report of the Committee to Study the Framework Hypothesis," Majority Report. Presbytery of Southern California (OPC). October 15-16, 1999.
Mathews	Mathews, Kenneth A. *Genesis 1—11:26.* Nashville: Broadman, 1996.
Pipa	Pipa, Joseph A., Jr. and David W. Hall, eds, *Did God Create in Six Days?* Taylors, S. C.: Southern Presbyterian, 1999.
Ramm	Ramm, Bernard. *The Christian View of Science and Scripture.* Grand Rapids: Eerdmans, 1955.
Ross	Ross, Mark, "The Framework Hypothesis," in Pipa (q.v.).
Sailhammer	Sailhammer, John H., "Genesis," in Frank E. Gaebelein, ed. *The Expositor's Bible Commentary.* Grand Rapids: Zondervan, 1990.
Shaw	Shaw, Benjamin, "The Literal Day Interpretation," in Pipa (q.v.).
Thompson	Thompson, J. A. "Genesis 1: Science? History? Theology?" *TSF Bulletin* 50 (Spring 1968): 12-23.
Thompson, "Creation"	Thompson. "Creation," in *New Bible Dictionary,* ed. J. D. Douglas, F. F. Bruce, *et al.* (Downers Grove, Ill.: InterVarsity, 1982), 245-47.

Van Gemeren	Van Gemeren, Willem. *The Progress of Redemption: The Story of Salvation from Creation to the New Jerusalem.* Grand Rapids: Zondervan, 1988.
Waltke	Waltke, Bruce K. "The Creation Account in Genesis 1:1-3. In five parts. *Bibliotheca Sacra* (Part I: January, 1975; Part II: April, 1975; Part III: July, 1975; Part IV: October, 1975; Part V: January, 1976).
Weeks	Weeks, Noel. *The Sufficiency of Scripture.* Edinburgh: Banner of Truth, 1988.
Wenham	Wenham, Gordon J. *Genesis 1-15.* Dallas: Word, 1987.
Young	Young, Edward J. *Studies in Genesis One.* Philadelphia: Presbyterian and Reformed, 1964.

PREFACE

The debate over Creation has never been a matter of disinterest in the contemporary Christian world. Nevertheless, it certainly has risen to a boiling point in recent years. For instance, a new approach to the Creation-Evolution debate has gained recent national media attention: the Intelligent Design argument.[1] This view is causing controversy not only among evolutionists, but even among traditional, biblical creationists. Christian astrophysicist Hugh Ross has recently become quite popular in his defense of the Bible from the Progressive Creationist perspective, which endorses evolutionary time scales in creation.[2]

Though not as widely known as the Intelligent Design or Progressive Creation approaches, within evangelical circles a seventy-five year old view of biblical Creation is at last beginning to make headway in the debate: the Framework Hypothesis. This view is enjoying the most influence in conservative and evangelical circles known for their commitment to Reformed theology and the Westminster Confession of Faith. However, it is receiving a hearing outside of Reformed circles.

Our book introduces the Framework Hypothesis to those who are not familiar with it. Intelligent Christians ought to keep abreast of such issues impacting the integrity of the faith and the Christian apologetic. After all, are we not obliged to "bring every thought captive to the obedience of Christ" (2 Cor. 10:5)? We must be relevant to the world of theological debate if we are to promote the faith effectively. But our relevance does not require *compromise* of our commitments.

Our book grew out of papers that Mike Butler and I wrote for a long-standing presbytery debate in southern California in the Orthodox Presbyterian Church (a conservative Presbyterian denomination founded by J. Gresham Machen in the 1930s). Though some portions of the book are directly relevant to the OPC discussion and debate, the implications are

---

[1] See for example the debate in Tony Carnes, "Design Interference" *Christianity Today*, 44:14 (December 4, 2001): 20. Alan G. Padgett, "Creation by Design," in *Books & Culture*, 6:4 (July/August, 2000): 30. Scott Swanson, "Debunking Darwin," *Christianity Today*, 41:1 (Jan. 6, 1997): 64.

[2] The dangers inherent in his position have been noted by evangelical theologian William Lane Craig, "Hugh Ross's Extra-Dimensional Deity: A Review Article," *Journal of the Evangelical Theological Society*, 42:2 (June, 1999): 293-304.

much broader. We take on the debate with the Framework Hypothesis as it is directly impacting the Orthodox Presbyterian Church and its sister denomination, the Presbyterian Church in America. Nevertheless, this book should prove valuable to the wider Reformed community—and even the broader evangelical world—for we engage the issues not only on confessional matters, but on exegetical and theological grounds as well. Indeed, requests for our papers have poured in from across the nation, prompting us to put them in a formally published, easily accessible, and widely available format.

Within this work the reader will discover solid exegetical arguments for the traditional view of Creation: the literal, sequential six day creation viewpoint. In addition, he or she will discover a thorough analysis, critique, and rebuttal to the leading arguments of the Framework Hypothesis. These not only rebut the Framework Hypothesis as such, but more fully elucidate the implications of the traditional viewpoint.

We present this work to the evangelical and Reformed world in the hope of furthering the debate, while at the same time providing material to assist Christians committed to the traditional view. As Winston Churchill once observed: "Men often stumble over the truth, but they invariably pick themselves up and continue on." We pray that our careful presentation of the traditional view over against the Framework Hypothesis might confirm the historic position of the Church in the modern world.

The authors of *Yea, Hath God Said?* serve on the faculty of Westminster Classical College in Elkton, Maryland. Michael R. Butler (M.A., Philosophy, Claremont University) is Associate Professor of Philosophy and Kenneth L Gentry, Jr. (Th. D., Theology, Whitefield Theological Seminary) is Professor of Systematic Theology and Dean of Faculty. Westminster Classical College is committed to the traditional six day creation perspective as a key component in promoting a full-orbed Christian worldview. We are both ordained elders: Butler is a ruling elder in the Orthodox Presbyterian Church; Gentry is a minister in the Presbyterian Church in America. We present this work to the evangelical world as concerned evangelical Presbyterians.

Rev. Kenneth L. Gentry, Jr., Th.D.
Dean of Faculty and Professor of Systematic Theology
Westminster Classical College
Elkton, Maryland

PART I
INTRODUCTORY REMARKS

Chapter 1
THE FRAMEWORK HYPOTHESIS DEBATE
Kenneth L. Gentry, Jr.

Introduction

The Christian is confronted with the fundamentally important matter of creation immediately upon opening his Bible to its first chapter.[3] In Genesis 1 we possess the direct revelation of God through Moses[4] regarding the divine origin and forming of the material universe and the temporal order, the divine filling of the earth with all its flora and fauna, and the creation of man as the special image of God and high point of creation. Moses' presentation is historical, and, as Hamilton notes: "Genesis does *not* use the language of myth in its narration of the Creation story" (Hamilton, 130).

The Christian Church has historically understood the Genesis account as revealing that the creation of the world followed the chronological order of the narrative of chapter 1.[5] And until 1869 when the Day Age Theory first appeared (Blocher, 43; Ramm, 211), the traditional exegesis also held that the duration of the creative process transpired "in the space of six days," as our Confessional Standards put it (WCF 4:2; LC 15, 120; SC 9). As Charles Hodge puts it: "according to the generally received interpretation of the first chapter of Genesis, the process of creation was completed in six days."[6] Thus, Christians have generally accepted the creation narrative as presenting the actual sequential progress of creation

---

[3] For the significance of this doctrine, see: John Murray, "The Significance of the Doctrine of Creation," in *Collected Writings of John Murray*, vol. 1, *The Claims of Truth* (Edinburgh: Banner of Truth, 1976), ch. 44.

[4] In this book we accepts the traditional Mosaic authorship of Genesis 1 and 2, as per Young, 67 n59, as over against the doubts of some Framework advocates (e.g., Ridderbos, 17, 28).

[5] See for example the following ancient writers (references to *Ante-Nicene Fathers*): Barnabas (1:146); Irenaeus (1:551, 557); Theophilus (2:9); Victorinus (7:341); Methodius (6:333); *Disputation of Archelaus and Manes* (6:203).

[6] Charles Hodge, *Systematic Theology*, 3 vols. (Grand Rapids: Eerdmans, rep. 1973), 1:570.

over the span of six days of twenty-four hours duration each. Indeed, this is called the "traditional view" by advocates of the Framework Hypothesis:

•Henri Blocher: It is "the reading that enjoys the support of the majority throughout church history, notably that of the Reformers"(Blocher, 46).

•Meredith Kline speaks of the chronological sequence view which has "long been traditional." He notes that "these traditional interpretations continue to be dominant in orthodox circles"("Rain," 146).[7] He also speaks of "the more traditional types of exegesis"("Space and Time," 11). Even today, some forty years later, he laments: "advocacy of the literalist tradition, however, is as clamant as ever" ("Space and Time," 2).

•Irons refers to the "more traditional interpretations" which are "time-honored exegetical options" (Irons, 23).[8]

Non-framework advocates capitalize on this fact when responding to Framework advocacy:

•Carl F. H. Henry: "It is fair to say that six-day creationists, and not theistic evolutionsts, reflect what may be taken as the Christian tradition before the rise of modern science."[9]

•Bibza and Currid: "This interpretation has had the greatest support throughout the history of the church. The majority of the Reformers, for example, held this view."[10]

•Kelly: "Simply stated, the writer of Genesis meant to say what the historic Christian Church (until the mid-nineteenth century) believed he said" (Kelly, 43).

---

[7] Kline includes Day Age advocates in this "traditional" camp because they also allow the sequential nature of the events as recorded in Genesis 1.

[8] Unfortunately, these "time-honored exegetical options" are derided by some Framework advocates as "biblicist" (Muether and Waltke) and "a deplorable disservice to the cause of biblical truth" (Kline). See: John R. Muether in Will S. Barker and W. Robert Godfrey, *Theonomy: An Informed Critique* (Grand Rapids: Zondervan, 1990), 254. Kline, "Space and Time," 15 (n 47). Waltke, 4:338-39.

[9] Carl F. H. Henry, *God Who Stands and Stays* (Part Two), vol. 6 of *God, Revelation and Authority* (Waco, Tex.: Word, 1983), 142. Henry criticizes Noordtzij, Ridderbos, and Kline on pages 134-35.

[10] James Bibza and John D. Currid, "A Cosmology of History: From Creation to Consummation," in W. Andrew Hoeffecker, ed., *Universe, Society, and Ethics*, vol. 1, *Building a Christian Worldview* (Phillipsburg, N. J.: Presbyterian and Reformed, 1986), 44.

•Grudem notes of the Framework Hypothesis that "comparatively few evangelicals have adopted it."[11]

•David W. Hall: "The long history of biblical interpretation, and specifically the Westminster divines' written comments, endorse only one of the major cosmological views considered today: *They thought creation happened neither in an instant nor over a long period, but in the space of six normally understood days*" (Hall, 267).

Zöckler explains the change of views regarding the creation process which was effected after the Reformation period during the Enlightenment:

> In the period of the Reformation . . . the commentators began to keep more closely to the words of the biblical narrative, and to avoid more carefully any trace of allegorization. But there came a time when natural science felt called upon to construct a doctrine of creation; and from that moment, the middle of the eighteenth century, until our time, a more or less noisy controversy has gone on between the orthodox party of the Church and the radical students of natural philosophy.
>
> It was, in the beginning, chiefly from the science of geology that the arguments against the biblical representation were drawn. Evidences derived from the most authentic document (the earth itself), and by the most infallible method (scientific observation), were marched up to show, that, instead, of a creation in six days, there was, indeed, a progressive development through huge periods. the scriptural narrative was ridiculed as childish; and captious questions were put to those who still adhered to its very letters.[12]

And now today, with several reformed seminaries being the instrument of change, reformed Christianity is wrestling with the growing presence of the "Framework Hypothesis" which readily admits its non-traditional standing. What is this *non-traditional* view that is shaking Presbyterian presbyteries, denominations, and other like-minded communions? What are its problems that so many traditional Christians deem of great concern? Does the Framework Hypothesis comport with the Westminster Standards, which defines historic Presbyterianism? Finally, is the Hypothesis a tolerable option on the crowded scene of approaches to biblical origins?

---

[11] Wayne Grudem, *Systematic Theology: An Introduction to Biblical Doctrine* (Grand Rapids: Zondervan, 1994), 303.

[12] Otto Zöchler, "Creation," in Philip Schaff, ed., *Schaff-Herzog Encyclopedia of Religious Knowledge* (Chicago: Funk & Wagnalls, 1887), 1:569.

These are a few of the questions that the authors of the present work, along with other ministers, sought to resolve in the Minority Report of our presbytery's "Special Committee to evaluate the conformity of the Framework Hypothesis to the teaching of Scripture and the Westminster Standards."

Working Definition of Framework Hypothesis

As a portion of our Committee work the Framework members took the opportunity to define the Framework Hypothesis with a view to keeping the fundamental nature of the system under scrutiny and to avoid erroneous constructions. And although the definition "evolved" (!) over the course of our labors, we established a definition that was acceptable at least to the Framework advocates on the presbytery's Committee. The original definition was established by full Committee action on October 3, 1998; the amended and final version September 27, 1999 — just one week before the Majority Report was released to the Minority on the Committee and two weeks before the presbytery Report was due.

The Committee's definition reads as follows:

> The Framework Interpretation of Genesis 1:1 through 2:3 is the view which maintains that, while the six days of creation are normal solar days, the total picture of God's completing His creative work in a week of days is not to be taken literally, but functions as a literary framework for the creation narrative;

> and that the eight creative historical works of God have been arranged according to other than strictly sequential considerations, and that where there is sequential order it must be determined by factors other than the order of narration alone.[13]

Although this was the working definition for our Committee, the question of its universal applicability remains open. For example, Blocher a major and vigorous proponent of the Framework Hypothesis, presents a definition that is not as clear on the "eight creative historical works of God" (see further discussion on this problem in an analysis by Michael R. Butler

---

[13] The original definition we used for a year in our deliberations read in part: "The Framework Interpretation of Genesis 1:1 through 2:3 is the view which maintains that the days of the creation week are not normal solar days, but function as part of a literary framework for the creation narrative. . . ."

elsewhere in our book). Thus, his and perhaps other definitions may not be as carefully crafted for presbytery debates within our denomination. Blocher draws a clear distinction between a *literary* approach to Genesis 1 and a *literal* approach:

> The literary interpretation takes the form of the week attributed to the work of creation to be an artistic arrangement, a modest example of anthropomorphism that is not to be taken literally. The author's intention is not to supply us with a chronology of origins. It is possible that the logical order he has chosen coincides broadly with the actual sequence of the facts of cosmogony; but that does not interest him. He wishes to bring out certain themes and provide a theology of the sabbath. The text is composed as the author meditates on the finished work, so that we may understand how the creation is related to God, and what is its significance for mankind. (Blocher, 50)

Problematic History of the Framework Hypothesis

Blocher lists "the main proponents" of the Framework Hypothesis among evangelicals: "The pioneer, around 1930, was A. Noordtzij of the University of Utrecht, and since World War II the main proponents have been N. H. Ridderbos of Amsterdam, B. Ramm of California, M. G. Kline of New England, D. F. Payne of Britain and J. A. Thompson of Australia" (Blocher, 50). Grudem adds Ronald Youngblood to the list of Framework advocates (Grudem, 301 n67). We will be employing especially the writings of these men to fill out our argument.

Despite the long-standing tradition of orthodox exegesis, deeply-held conviction of Christian devotion, and (in reformed circles) the confessionally-secured affirmation of ministerial commitment, Genesis 1 is a flash point of debate in our present, post-Darwin world. In fact, in 1958 Meredith Kline, the putative mentor of American Framework advocacy, observed that "there are no signs that the debate over the chronological data of Genesis 1 is abating." There he noted that the debate's "flames have recently been vigorously fanned by the bellows of the dissenters" (Kline, "Rain," 146). The "dissenters" cited by Kline were Framework theologians Bernard Ramm and N. H. Ridderbos, whose "discussions in particular have evoked animated reactions among evangelicals" (Kline, "Rain," 146, n1).[14]

The impact of the creation debate appears to be increasing and has, of late, been seriously affecting the peace of the church in reformed circles. In fact, within the conservative Reformed communions of the Orthodox Presbyterian Church, the Presbyterian Church in America, and the Reformed Church in the United States the debate appears to be reaching a crescendo, resulting primarily from the spread of the Framework Hypothesis.

The Reformed Church in the United States has specifically declared it will not license or ordain candidates who hold the Framework Hypothesis. Indeed, a 1985 resolution stated: "that the Eureka Classis, Reformed Church in the United States, register a protest against the teaching at Westminster Theological Seminary in California and Philadelphia, which questions the chronological sequence of the six normal days of light and darkness in Genesis one. We believe that this skeptical interpretation of holy Scripture is dangerous to the faith and theology of the students and to the churches which these students shall serve."

Framework proponent Lee Irons well-expresses the problem regarding our own ecclesiastical setting, when he confesses: "the position known as 'the framework hypothesis' has been at the center of considerable controversy recently in certain sectors of the OPC." In his footnote he correctly surmises that "the Framework Hypothesis seems to be a potential source of division in the PCA as well," noting "the depth of the conflict" (Irons, 2).

At least one presbytery in the PCA (Westminster Presbytery in Tennessee and Virginia) takes a similar stance to that of the RCUS. On April 18, 1998 this presbytery passed a declaration on creation and concluded with the following words:

> Westminster Presbytery does declare and make known to the world and to all churches … that we will not tolerate these views [the Framework Hypothesis, among others] in any teaching elder seeking admittance to this Presbytery, or any other man seeking to be licensed to be a candidate for the ministry under care of the this Presbytery. Furthermore, Westminster Presbytery considers that any view which departs from the

---

[14] See also: Young, 44, 55.

confessional doctrines of creation in six, 24-hour days strikes at the fundamentals of the system of doctrine set forth in the Holy Scriptures.

In the Orthodox Presbyterian Church setting, The Credentials Committee of the Presbytery of Northern California (OPC) took the position that before an advocate of the Framework Hypothesis may be licensed or ordained, he must acknowledge his exception to the Westminster Confession (declare he is out of accord with the confession of the church at that point) and must not promote his "private view," so that the purity and unity of the church might be guarded.

Because of the growing controversy surrounding the Framework Hypothesis, the Presbytery of Southern California of the Orthodox Presbyterian Church appointed a "Special Committee to Evaluate the Framework Hypothesis"at its stated meeting in May of 1998. Consequently, the presbytery's task was both significant and relevant; the Committee labor had serious implications for the ongoing life and health of the church. And this on a crucial issue of our witness to the world: our view of creation, which is directly opposed by the religion of modern man, evolutionary theory.[15]

Although Irons proposes that we abandon the label "Framework Hypothesis" in favor of his preferred designation "framework interpretation," in our paper and in our book we continued employing the former. Though our choice of labels may be little more than a quibble, we maintain it in that: (1) This is the familiar designation that has prevailed at least since Ridderbos' seminal work defending it and E. J. Young's classic refutation.[16] (2) Recent Framework advocates employ it without hesitation, for example, Tremper Longman, Henri Blocher, and Mark E. Ross,[17] as do

---

[15] For a summary argument of evolution as a faith commitment, see: Kelly, 37-39. For a fuller treatment: Phillip Johnson, *Evolution as Dogma: The Establishment of Naturalism* (Dallas: Haughton, 1990).

[16] Ridderbos, 36, 38, 40, 41, 42, 45, 54, 56, 68, etc. Young, 44, 55.

[17] Tremper Longman III, "Literary Approaches to Biblical Interpretation," in Moises Silva, ed., *Foundations of Contemporary Interpretation* (Grand Rapids: Zondervan, 1996), 130. Blocher, "In the Beginning," 50, 53. Blocher also calls it the "framework theory," 49. Ross, 113, 114, 117, 119.

most contemporary critics.[18] (3) The Presbytery of Southern California originally appointed the Committee to "evaluate the conformity of the Framework Hypothesis to the teaching of Scripture and the Westminster Confession and Catechisms" (Minutes, May 22-23, 462). The Majority Report itself spoke of the framework of triad structure as an "hypothesis" (Majority Report, 6, 7). (5) The Minority on the Committee did not deem the Framework approach to Genesis 1 a justifiable interpretation. At best, it is a working hypothesis that goes contrary to "traditional" exegesis (as admitted by Framework advocates themselves).

We must point out at this early stage in the development of the argument that we are not tenaciously holding to an approach to Scripture more in keeping with a naive fundamentalism. Rather our position stands upon the exegetical observations of well-argued, long-standing, traditional orthodoxy (e.g., C. F. Keil, H. C. Leupold[19]), including many notable reformed scholars:

•Martin Luther asserts "that Moses spoke in the literal sense, not allegorically or figuratively, i.e., that the world, with all its creatures, was created within six days, as the words read."[20]

•John Calvin concludes "that God himself took the space of six days" to create; and that "six days were employed in the formation of the world."[21]

•Our own Westminster Standards declare that God created the world "in the space of six days" (WCF 4:2; LC 120; SC 9), "within the space of six days" (LC 15).

---

[18] Weeks, "hypothesis" (104, 108, 115), "theory" (105, 112). John D. Currid in Hoffecker, *Building a Christian Worldview*, 2:46. Wayne Grudem, *Systematic Theology: An Introduction to Biblical Doctrine* (Grand Rapids: Zondervan, 1994), "hypothesis" (301), "theory" (302). See also Pipa, *passim*.

[19] Keil and Delitzsch. H. C. Leupold, *Exposition of Genesis*, 2 vols. (Grand Rapids: Baker, 1970).

[20] Martin Luther, *Lectures on Genesis: Chapters 1-5*, trans. George V. Schick, vol. 1 of *Luther's Works*, ed. Jaroslav Pelikan (St. Louis: Concordia, 1958), 1:5. Cited from Conrad Hyers, *The Meaning of Creation: Genesis and Modern Science* (Richmond, Vir.: John Knox, 1984), 5.

[21] John Calvin, *Commentaries of the First Book of Moses Called Genesis*, trans. John King (Grand Rapids: Eerdmans, 1948), 1:78, 105.

•John Gill explains that "though God took six days for the creation of the world and all things in it, to make his works the more observable, and that they might be distinctly considered, and gradually become the object of contemplation and wonder; yet the work of every day, and every particular work in each day, were done in a moment, without any motion and change, without any labour and fatigue, only by a word speaking, by an almighty *fiat*, let it be done, and it immediately was done."[22]

•Francis Turretin, in rebutting Augustine's instantaneous creation view, holds that "the simple and historical Mosaic narration . . . mentions six days and ascribes a particular work to each day."[23]

•Robert L. Dabney argues that "the sacred writer seems to shut us up to the literal interpretation," noting that "the natural day is its literal and primary meaning" (Dabney, 255).

•Geerhardus Vos observes that "the days of creation were ordinary days."[24]

•Louis Berkhof vigorously argues that "the literal interpretation of the term 'day' in Gen. 1 is favored" (Berkhof, 154).

•Heinrich Heppe explains that "God completed the creation of matter and of the creatures made from it in the course of six successive days; not as though God could not have called every item into existence in one moment, but in order to manifest the variety and wise ordering of His creatures."[25]

•Jack Scott, former Professor of Old Testament, Reformed Theological Seminary, Jackson, affirms of the days of Genesis "the Biblical order of the 24 hour period."[26]

•Douglas Kelly, Professor of Systematic Theology, Reformed Theological Seminary, Charlotte, in his book length defense of the traditional exegesis,

---

[22] John Gill, *A Body of Divinity* (Grand Rapids: Sovereign Grace, 1971 [rep. 1769]), 261.

[23] Francis Turretin, *Institutes of Elenctic Theology*, trans. George Musgrave Giger, edited by James T. Dennison, Jr. (Phillipsburg, N. J.: P & R Publishing, rep. 1992), 1:444.

[24] From his *Gereformeerde Dogmatiek*, as cited in Louis Berkhof, *Systematic Theology* (Grand Rapids: Eerdmans, 1941), 154.

[25] Heinrich Heppe, *Reformed Dogmatics: Set Out and Illustrated from the Sources*, ed. Ernst Bizer, trans. G. T. Thomson (Grand Rapids: Baker, 1978 [rep. 1950], 199.

[26] Jack B. Scott, *God's Plan Unfolded* (n.p., 1976), 9.

provides various reasons why we must understand the "Genesis 'days' as plain, solar days" (Kelly, 109).

•Robert L. Reymond, Professor of Systematic Theology, Knox Theological Seminary, informs us that he "can discern no reason, either from Scripture or from the human sciences, for departing from the view that the days of Genesis were ordinary twenty-four-hour days."[27]

•Morton H. Smith, Professor of Systematic and Biblical Theology; Joseph A. Pipa, President; Benjamin Shaw, Associate Professor of Old Testament; Sid Dyer, Associate Professor of Greek and New Testament (all at Greenville Presbyterian Theological Seminary) and W. Duncan Rankin, Associate Professor of Systematic Theology, Reformed Theological Seminary, are contributors to a book-length defense of the historical exegesis and confessional of Genesis 1: *Did God Create in Six Days?* (Pipa, *passim*).

Traditionalist Concerns with the Framework Hypothesis

Below in Chapter 2 I will summarize the exegetical evidence for a literal, sequential six day creation, as long held in the history of Christianity. In Chapter 3 I will critique the leading arguments buttressing the Framework Hypothesis. But at this juncture I will briefly list a few of the concerns that traditionalist interpreters have with non-literal approaches to Genesis 1 (such as the Framework Hypothesis). Although some of these may appear to commit the consequentialist fallacy, the concerns are real and deserve due reflection. (Due to our ecclesiastical setting within evangelical orthodoxy, we will avoid citing and interacting with overtly liberal advocates of the Framework Hypothesis, such as Conrad Hyers.[28])

---

[27] Robert L. Reymond, *A New Systematic Theology of the Christian Faith* (Nashville: Thomas Nelson, 1998), 392.

[28] Conrad Hyers, *The Meaning of Creation: Genesis and Modern Science* (Atlanta: John Knox, 1984), see especially Parts II and IV. Evangelical commentator Kenneth Mathews lists Hyers along with Blocher as advocates "for the Framework' ('Literary') view." Matthews, *Genesis 1-11:26*, 107 (n 206). See Hyer's triad chart: "Problem, Preparation, Population," 69.

Exegetical Concerns

The Framework Hypothesis Discounts Obvious Textual Indicators. Though *prima facie* considerations may often collapse upon closer analysis, the fact is that most evangelicals admit the first impression impact of the historically accepted exegesis of Genesis 1. We may at least argue that such *prima facie* evidence places the burden of proof on those who would discount it, especially when set within the context of long-standing traditional exegesis — Irons' strained attempt at reversing the burden notwithstanding (Irons, 53).

Charles Hodge confesses that "it is of course admitted that, taking this account by itself, it would be most natural to understand the word [*yom*] in its ordinary sense."[29] Dabney observes that "the plain reader has no trouble with it" (Dabney, 255). Framework critic E. J. Young notes that "if we read Genesis 'without prepossession or suspicion' we receive the impression that the author meant to teach a creation in six ordinary days and, more than that, to teach that the earth was created before the sun, moon and stars. This impression, apparently, is to be considered naive." E. J. Young warns that such charges of naivete "prove too much, for it could be applied to other passages of Scripture as well. One who reads the Gospels, for example, is likely to receive the impression that they teach that Jesus rose from the dead. But can we in this day of science seriously be expected to believe that such an event really took place?" (Young, 66, 67).

Against various non-chronological views, including J. A. Thompson's Framework perspective, Derek Kidner objects: "Yet to the present writer the march of the days is too majestic a progress to carry no implication of ordered sequence; it also seems over-subtle to adopt a view of the passage which discounts one of the primary impressions it makes on the ordinary reader" (Kidner, *Genesis*, 54-55). Day Age proponent R. L. Harris "will freely admit, that the view that the days were 24-hour days is a natural first reading of the chapter, especially in English" (Harris, 21).

Indeed, Framework advocates themselves admit this. Ridderbos confesses that "one who reads Genesis 1 without prepossession or suspicion is almost bound to receive the impression that the author's intent is to say that creation took place in six ordinary days" (Ridderbos, 29). Mark Ross

---

[29] Hodge, *Systematic Theology*, 1:570-71.

agrees: "It is admitted by all that the first impression of Genesis 1:1— 2:3 is of a sequential, chronological account of a six day creation with a seventh day of rest" (Ross, 118).

Against not only the admitted historical tradition, the universally acknowledged first impression, the careful numerical succession of days defined by evening and morning — and many other such exegetical observations (see Chapter 2 below) — Framework theologian Blocher declares "the text gives not the slightest hint" of the literal interpretation! Remarkably, he declares "there is no reason to suppose it"! (Blocher, 52, 53). Thompson agrees: "It is difficult to see how this great chapter was ever intended to become anything other than a tremendous affirmation of the fact that God is the creator of all things" (Thompson, 22). Irons concurs: "the text contains so many indications that its chronological data are *not* to be taken literally that it truly puzzles us that we non-literalists are always having to shoulder the *onus probadi*. In all candor we believe that the literalist interpretation has the burden of proof in this case" (Irons, 53).

With such strong assertions one must wonder why the sequential interpretation enjoyed, as Blocher informs us, "the support of the majority throughout church history, notably that of the Reformers" (Blocher, 46). Why, according to Irons, are *sequential* approaches "the traditional interpretations" (Irons, 23)? It would appear from the observations of Blocher, Thompson, and Irons that the *one and only* temporal conclusion we may draw from the text is that it does *not* teach that God created the world in the space of six days — despite the express, vivid, chronological, enumerated order of the narrative. This conclusion is incredible, and fuels our burning suspicions about the danger of the Framework Hypothesis method for other historical texts.

The Framework Hypothesis Relies on Extravagant Theological Analysis. In discounting the *prima facie* impression of the Genesis 1 account of creation, the Framework Hypothesis establishes in its place a complex, counter-intuitive hermeneutical approach. We will provide a somewhat fuller critique of the Framework methodology in Chapter 3; here I simply highlight the *prima facie* difficulty of the Framework method.

In 1996 Kline published an important article titled: "Space and Time in the Genesis Cosmogony." He wrote it because "an apologia is needed for addressing again the question of the chronological data in the Genesis creation account." This article presents his "two-register cosmological concept" which has "developed into the main point and has become the umbrella under which the other, restated arguments are accorded an ancillary place here and there" (Kline, "Space and Time," 2). According to Framework advocate Irons, "Kline's 1996 article is the most comprehensive and convincing exegetical defense of the framework interpretation available" (Irons, 36).

But what do we discover upon reading Kline's presentation? What does Kline offer in the place of the historic, confessional, *prima facie* impression of Genesis 1? Jack Collins, associate professor of Old Testament at Covenant Theological Seminary, an expert in discourse analysis and language theory and himself a non-literalist, complains that Kline's article is "quite complicated and hard to follow, even for the biblical specialist."[30] And this is despite Kline's presenting it as a "more accessible statement" of his "exegetical arguments" (Kline, "Space and Time," 1)! Kelly declares such exegesis "a tortured mode of interpretation" (Kelly, 119).

If Kline's extravagance is true, we must conclude that not only were the ancient Jewish people not in the least naive, but they held highly sophisticated and intricate theories of textual expression — hidden beneath the veil of simple historical narrative. But as Cassuto observes regarding Genesis 1: it "was not intended for the thinkers and the elect few only, but for the people as a whole, including also its common folk" (Cassuto, 12). Even Framework advocate Thompson writes: "If such a book is to find acceptance among all peoples (which incidentally, it does), its language in regard to natural phenomena must be simple, popular, and understandable to all" (Thompson, 14; cp. p. 22). He further warns: "One must always avoid the temptation of forcing the symbols into a complex maze of theological speculations" (Thompson, 15). Well stated!

Anyone who has labored through Kline's prior *Images of the Spirit* (1980) knows the chore before him. His "Space and Time in the Genesis Cosmogony" provides further evidence that Kline, as Blocher puts it, is "not afraid to leave the beaten track." And this is just the latest in a series of unique arguments for the Framework Hypothesis, for as Blocher also notes

---

[30] Jack B. Collins, "Response to Kline," *Perspectives on Science and Christian Faith*, 48:2 (June 1996): 141.

of Kline's 1957 article based on Genesis 2:5: he "has thrown into the arena a new argument" (Blocher, 53). Kline disciple Mark Futato confesses that he himself offers "new insights" which have "not yet been set forth" (Futato, 1, 2). The hypothetical nature of the Framework approach is evidenced in its constant creation of new insights never before seen in the history of exegesis.

Furthermore, some advocates of the Framework Hypothesis assert that Genesis employs images from ancient cosmogonies, effectively picking up on the errors of antiquity and reporting them as truth. For instance, Ridderbos writes:

> And with regard to verses 6ff. one can say that the author expresses himself in terms derived from the world-picture of the ancient Orient, or to put it differently, in the terminology current in his day. The ancient orient generaly [*sic*] held to the concept of a celestial arch which separated the waters above, the heavenly ocean from the waters beneath (cf. also Gen. 7:11, 8:2, Ps. 148:4, Is. 24:18). (Ridderbos, 44[31])

By applying literary analysis based on the opposition between ancient pagan and the Jewish cosmogonies, Framework advocate Waltke[32] promotes a flawed and dangerous view of Genesis 1:2 when he declares it represents the "situation prior to the creation" (Waltke, 2:28). He argues of the "primeval, dark, watery, and formless state prior to creation" that Genesis does not attribute "this state to the Creator/creator" (Waltke, 4:329). And: "ברא [*bara*] in Genesis 1:1 does not include the bringing into existence of the negative state described in verse 2" (Waltke, 4:336). He continues:

> But what about the uncreated or unformed state, the darkness and the deep of Genesis 1:2? Here a great mystery is encountered, for the Bible never

---

[31] See also: Hyers, *The Meaning of Creation*, 39. Hyers is a liberal proponent of the Framework Hypothesis.

[32] Waltke designates the Six Days of creation as a "temporal framework" with the first three days paralleling the last three. Waltke, 4:341; 5:29-31. He is deemed a Framework proponent by Metaphorical Day advocate Collins in Pipa, 146. In an e-mail to Ken Gentry dated October 6, 1999, Irons doubts this classification: "I would have to say that his position should not be classified as the framework interpretation." Waltke does, however, appear to hold to the fundamental elements of the Framework Hypothesis according to our Committee definition.

says that God brought these into existence by His word. What, then, can be said about them?

First, it can be said that the Book of Genesis does not inform us concerning the origin of that which is contrary to the nature of God, neither in the cosmos nor in the world of the spirit. . . .

The biblicist faces a dilemma when considering the origin of those things which are contrary to God. A good God characterized by light could not, in consistency with His nature, create evil, disorder, and darkness. On the other hand, it cannot be eternally outside of Him for that would limit His sovereignty. The Bible resolves the problem not be explaining its origin but by assuring man that it was under the dominion of the Spirit of God. (Waltke, 4:338-39)

Later he surmises:

Moreover, to show His sovereign dominion over His creation, God gave names to the light, to the darkness, to the firmament, to the dry land, and to the gathered waters. He called them Day, Night, Heavens, Earth, and Sea, respectively. To understand the significance of this act of naming the parts of the creation it must be realized that in the Semitic world the naming of something or someone was the token of lordship. . . . Is it not significant that God gave names precisely to those features that belonged to the precreated situation? In so doing He showed that He was Lord of all. (Waltke, 4:341)

Still later, in his study of the wisdom analysis of creation in Proverbs 8, Waltke muses: "Many commentators assume that the 'depths' spoken of in verse 24 refer to the תהום [*tehom*] mentioned in Genesis 1:2. If this is so, then wisdom is including the state mentioned in Genesis 1:2 as among God's creative acts, and the present writer's analysis of Genesis 1:1-3 must be wrong" (Waltke, 5:38).

The Framework Hypothesis Promotes a Dangerous Hermeneutic. The Framework Hypothesis approaches the foundational chapter of Genesis, which is the cornerstone of all Scripture, in a way that *can* easily lead to dismissing it from the realm of historical factuality. Those of us who served on the original presbytery Committee were pleased that the Framework advocates on the presbytery strongly affirmed the factual nature of the several divine creative works in Genesis 1. But we believed that such is held on a tenuous basis *given the tolerances within their literary theory*. I will

15

present one sample from a noted Framework proponent to illustrate our concern (other illustrations may be found later in this book).

While dealing with "history recording in the Bible" as an introduction to his Framework analysis of Genesis 1, Thompson writes:

> The point should be clear. Within the pages of the Old Testament there are many ways of recording historical events. To be sure, the normal method of recording history is either the annalistic or the selective with interpretive comments. But there are a significant number of cases where the language is figurative or symbolic enough indeed to show that the figurative, the symbolic, the descriptive form of presentation was an acceptable medium in Israel for recording the historical events, particularly when it was not so much the intimate details of the event that mattered, but some broad, underlying issue which could be emphasized and highlighted by a parable, a fable, or a vivid presentation in highly figurative language.
>
> I have laboured this point because it is important for the proposition that *in Genesis 1-3 we are dealing with events*, the exact nature of which may escape us as to detail, but the fact of which, and the import of which for all future generations of men, are by no means obscured by the symbols, and by the figurative and descriptive language used in their presentation.
>
> There is another important aspect of this argument. It is that, while men might freely use symbolism and figurative language for events which were well known and for which the details could be obtained from written records or from eye-witnesses, it was impossible to call on witnesses or written records either for the dawn of human history or for its end. In the realm of the *proton* or the *eschaton*, the use of symbolic and figurative language was the only possible way of approach. (Thompson, 17)

On what necessary principle may we declare that when dealing with matters regarding the original creative activity of God "the use of symbolic and figurative language was the only possible way of approach" (Thompson, 17)? The "only possible way"? Certainly when dealing with cosmic origins the only sure insights we may gain will be from divine revelation, since man was not present. But since God created the orderly, objective, physical world, why is a figurative approach the *only* possible approach? This simply does not make sense. This is a non sequitur of the most glaring sort, despite it being an "important aspect" of the Framework Hypothesis, according to Thompson. If God created the world either in an instant, or in six days, or over billions of years, why is not "possible" for him to so inform us? These and other results of the literary approach to Genesis 1 alarm adherents to the historic and confessional exegesis of the text, and seem not only unnecessarily extravagant but exegetically unwarranted and theologically perilous.

Theological Concerns

The Framework Hypothesis Reinterprets Implications of Divine Curse. The Framework Hypothesis demands a creational process consuming billions of years, for as Kline argues: "with respect to both the duration and sequence of events, the scientist is left free of biblical constraints in hypothesizing about cosmic origins" (Kline, "Space and Time," 2). Not only does this teach us that God has only "recently" completed his creation,[33] but a consequence of this is that "according to natural science there were great catastrophes, caused by movements of the earth-crust, there was cruelty and the 'struggle for life' long before man appeared and hence *a fortiori* before the fall" (Ridderbos, 70).[34] Thus, not only do chaos, destruction, and death precede by countless eons the curse of God, but they are actually features of God's creative activity, which was "very good" (Ge 1:31).

What is more, Kline states that "the Bible does not require us, therefore, to think of the character and working of man's natural environment before the Fall as radically different from what is presently the case."[35] This effectively discounts the enormity of God's curse which prevails over all creation and explains death in the animal world. Numerous arguments demand, however, that animal death results from God's curse on creation

---

[33] The universe is supposedly 12 billion years old; man (the last created entity during the original period of divine creative activity, Mt 19:4; Mk 10:6) is no more than 3 illion years old. Oddly, on this view and with Kline's assumptions, the second coming of Christ could end temporal history at (in Kline's view) "any moment." Were Christ to return today, 15 billion years would have expired in the creation process, and *at the most* 3 million years since the end of creation (but really much, much less, according to natural science estimations). That is, less than .002 per cent of earth's history would involve man, God's highest creature!

[34] See also: Blocher, 42, and Thompson, 34.

[35] Meredith G. Kline, *Kingdom Prologue* (S. Hamilton, Mass.: self-published, 1991), 81.

after Adam's fall, rather than being a feature of God's original creational activity:

First, by divine decree man and animals were herbivorous originally. In Genesis 1:29-30 God grants only vegetation for food, for both man *and* animals. As Hamilton notes regarding man's dominion over the animals: "such dominion does not allow him to kill these creatures or to use their flesh as food. Only much later (9:3, post-Flood) is domination extended to include consumption" (Hamilton, 139). He continues: "Man is to have as his food the seed and fruit of plants. Animals and birds are to have the leaves. . . . At no point is anything (human beings, animals, birds) allowed to take the life of another living being and consume it for food. . . . What is strange, and probably unexplainable (from a scientific position), is the fact that the animals too are not carnivores but also vegetarians" (Hamilton, 140; cp. Wenham, 33). Despite this, Framework advocates do not suggest that animals were vegetarians for hundreds of millions of years.

Second, the "death" of vegetation is of a qualitatively different order, and not as a result of divine curse, for: (1) God expressly designs vegetation alone for food consumption (Ge 1:29-30). (2) Plants lack a נֶפֶשׁ *nephesh*, unlike animal and man (Ge 1:20, 24, 30; 2:7). In fact, both animal (Ge 1:20-21, 24; 9:10) and man (Ge 2:7) are called "living creatures" (נֶפֶשׁ הַיָּה , *nephesh hayah*). Of Genesis 1:20-24, Waltke explains: "Man is here being associated with the other creatures as sharing in the passionate experience of life and is not being defined as distinct from them."[36] (3) Plants do not possess the "breath (רֽוּחַ, *ruach*) of life," as do animals and man (Ge 6:17; 7:15, 22). (4) Scripture never ponders the loss of a plant's *ruach*, as it does animal's and man's (Ecc 3:20); in fact, a similarity exists between man's *ruach* and animal's (Ecc 3:19). (5) When animal life "returns to the dust" it is because God "hides his face" (Ps 104:29).

Third, the creation account does not record God's "blessing" creation until the creation of *sentient* life on Day 5 (Ge 1:22). By this means of blessing, God draws a distinction between the zoological and the botanical orders of life. In that "blessing" often implies fecundity — which *plants* also have (Ge 1:11-12) — the lack of God's "blessing" plant life indicates this divine benediction is *more* than endowing living organisms with the capacity to multiply (contra Kline, "Space and Time," 6; Irons, 28).

---

[36] Bruce K. Waltke, *nephesh*, in *Theological Wordbook of the Old Testament*, 2:590.

Fourth, Paul relates the effects of the curse upon the creation in such a way that surely implies that the post-fall creation must be quite different from the original, uncursed world. He even strongly suggests that animal death is a consequence of it: "For the creation was *subjected to futility*, not of its own will, but because of Him who subjected it, in hope that the creation itself also will be set free from its *slavery to corruption* into the freedom of the glory of the children of God. For we know that *the whole creation groans and suffers* the pains of childbirth together until now" (Ro 8:20-23). Note that this "slavery to corruption" and "groaning and suffering" result from God's "subjecting creation to futility" — obviously by divine curse.

In fact, according to Larger Catechism 29: "The punishments of sin in this world are either inward, as blindness of mind, a reprobate sense, strong delusions, hardness of heart, horror of conscience, and vile affections; or outward, as *the curse of God upon the creatures* for our sakes, and all other evils that befall us in our bodies, names, estates, relations, and employments; together with death itself." According to Murray, the bondage of corruption in the creation itself (Ro 8:21) "must be taken in the sense of the decay and death apparent even in non-rational creation."[37] (For more information on this matter see later arguments.)

The Framework Hypothesis Opens the Possibility of Evolutionary Theory. Many Framework advocates clearly disavow evolution; we applaud their resolute stand against this heinous theory. Nevertheless, we are concerned are over the theoretical tolerance of evolution which the Framework Hypothesis allows — and which we believe cannot be resisted on the principles inherent in the Hypothesis.

Our concerns illustrated: Early on in the American spread of the Framework Hypothesis an uneasy suspicion arose that the theory was generated to allow for the "assured results" of naturalistic scientific theory. Young expresses his concern thus: "recently there has appeared a recrudescence of the so-called 'framework' hypothesis of the days of Genesis, an hypothesis which in the opinion of the writer of this article treats the content of Genesis one too lightly and which, at least according

---

[37] John Murray, *The Epistle to the Romans* (Grand Rapids: Eerdmans, 1965), 1:304.

to some of its advocates, seems to rescue the Bible from the position of being in conflict with the data of modern science" (Young, 44). Later he writes that "some of those who espouse a non-chronological view of the days of Genesis are moved by a desire to escape the difficulties which exist between Genesis and the so-called 'findings' of science" (Young, 51). After considering the wealth of exegetical evidence for the traditional view of Genesis 1, he writes under the heading "The Real Problem in Genesis One": "It is questionable whether serious exegesis of Genesis one would in itself lead anyone to adopt a non-chronological view of the days for the simple reason that everything in the text militates against it. Other considerations, it would seem, really wield a controlling influence. As it stands Genesis might be thought to conflict with 'science'" (Young, 100).

This suspicion continues today. Weeks expresses his alarm: "While some authors claim to be interpreting Genesis with never a thought about the views of dominant secular science, such claims are rather unconvincing. Obviously a conviction that the majority of scientist cannot be wrong must lead to a disposition towards non-literal interpretations" (Weeks, 96-97). Kelly surmises that "it must be some factor from outside the Scripture itself that has caused distinguished Christian exegetes to bring in such a tortured mode of interpretation" (Kelly, 119). Grudem notes that "one aspect of the attractiveness of this theory is the fact that it relieves evangelicals of the burden of even trying to reconcile scientific findings with Genesis 1" (Grudem, 302).

Our concerns justified: Ridderbos' title certainly suggests such a motive: *Is There A Conflict Between Genesis 1 and Natural Science?* This is especially so when we realize that evolution is a major conclusion of contemporary "natural science," indeed, the controlling principle guiding natural science today. A leading problem he has with a literal construction of Genesis 1 is that there "arise grave difficulties with respect to natural science" (Ridderbos, 46). Kline accepts the conclusions of naturalistic scientific inquiry as a given when he sympathizes with Ridderbos' concerns: "surely natural revelation concerning the sequence of developments in the universe as a whole and the sequence of the appearance of the various orders of life on our planet (unless the revelation has been completely misinterpreted) would require the exegete to incline to a not exclusively chronological interpretation of the creation week" (Kline, "Rain," 157).

In fact, more recently Kline complains: "I am unable to accept the strictly chronological interpretation of Genesis 1 when I take account of the light of natural revelation concerning the sequence of the primordial events"; and "the more traditional interpretations of the creation account are guilty not only of creating a conflict between the Bible and science but, in effect, of pitting Scripture against Scripture" (Kline, "Space and Time," 13). He speaks of the "aeons of creation" as a given fact (Kline, "Rain," 115).

Framework advocate Blocher criticizes the traditionalist view of a literal six day creation as engaging in "anti-scientism" (Blocher, 22, 48, 224, 227, etc.). He queries: "How are we to compare the assertion of the seven days with the billions of years, at the lowest estimate, which current scientific theory attributes to the origin of the universe?" He admits but tries to avoid the implications of our concerns by noting the great advantage of adapting to contemporary scientific conclusions: "So great is the advantage, and for some the relief, that it could constitute a temptation."And yet he confesses that the Framework Hypothesis provides a positive benefit in relieving us of "the confrontation with the scientific vision of the most distant past" (Blocher, 50).

Of the six literal day view of Genesis 1 Framework exegete Wenham[38] laments "the result that science and Scripture have been pitted against each other instead of being seen as complementary" (Wenham, 39).

Even more pointedly Kline confesses: "In this article I have advocated an interpretation of biblical cosmogony according to which Scripture is open to the current scientific view of a very old universe and, in that respect, does not discountenance the theory of the evolutionary origin of man" (Kline, "Space and Time," 15, n 47). Fortunately, he holds that Genesis 2:7 discourages an evolutionary view of human origins. Nevertheless, on Kline's own words he has "advocated an interpretation of biblical cosmogony" that allows "the evolutionary origin of man." And since he hesitates here solely on the basis of his exposition of Genesis 2:7 and Luke 3:38, and since these verses do not refer to animal origins, obviously he himself is very much open to biotic evolution short of man.

---

[38] Collins classifies Wenham as a Framework advocate in Pipa, 146. Irons states regarding the Framework definition: "I would argue that anyone who holds to a position that meets these two criteria holds to the framework interpretation" (Irons, 3). Wenham holds that the days are a part of a literary "framework" allowing a "six-day schema" designed simply to "stress the system and order that has been built into creation." Wenham, 7, 39.

Even here with Genesis 2:7 serving as an exegetical brake, we must wonder — given Kline's literary approach — if this verse might simply inform us of nothing more than God's special interest in and intimate concern for man, and not provide us with a literal description of man's origin. Blocher surmises that in composing Genesis Moses merely "wishes to bring out certain themes and provide a theology of the sabbath" (Blocher, 50). Thompson informs us that historical narratives such as Genesis 1 can be presenting "some broad, underlying issue which could be emphasized and highlighted by a parable, a fable, or a vivid presentation in highly figurative language" (Thompson, 17). Therefore, *conceivably* upon the Framework hermeneutic, Moses could be providing us a more general, theological explanation of man's origin in Genesis 2:7. After all, current scientific theory teaches that man *ultimately* derives from the "dust," tracing his ancestry back to single-celled, land-based organisms evolving into more complex entities.

Thompson, however, is not as cautious as Kline. He claims ignorance regarding the possibility of the evolutionary origin of man: "The picture of man is a noble one. But despite the nobility of the picture, all that we are told about the origin of man is that God 'made' him and God 'created' him. How God performed His work is not declared. Hence, provided that we are persuaded of the fact that man, like everything else in the universe, is the work of God, it would seem that in our present state of knowledge, we must allow for diversity of opinion among Christians. So far as I am aware the scientists do not know the origin of man. An attitude of reverent agnosticism is the only reasonable attitude to adopt" (Thompson, 21).

Furthermore, perhaps the rather unscientific, non-providential view of Eve's origin might merely be a literary device instructing us of the divinely blessed *unity* between husband and wife. Perhaps *both* Adam's and Eve's origins are literary artifices teaching this, and nothing more. We must remember the "genius" of Moses in composing Genesis 1, according to Framework advocates: "The text is composed as the author meditates on the finished work, so that we may understand how the creation is related to God, and what is its significance for mankind" (Blocher, 50). Framework proponent Thompson[39] agrees: "The primary importance of Genesis 1-3 lies not in any specific historical or scientific value, but in their theological value; that is, in their great assertions about the nature of God, man and the world" (Thompson, 13). Why should not the exegetico-theological method of the Framework Hypothesis surmise a related rationale for these — unusual and primitive? — features of Genesis 2? Especially since both Adam's and Eve's creation involve an "unnecessary supernaturalism," to use Kline's remarkable concept (Kline, "Rain," 150)?

And what about the temptation of Eve by the serpent in Genesis 3? Surely *here* we have some sort of parable, it would seem! After all, does not Framework advocate Thompson instruct us: "But there are a significant number of cases where the language is figurative or symbolic enough indeed to show that the figurative, the symbolic, the descriptive form of presentation was an acceptable medium in Israel for recording the historical events, particularly when it was not so much the intimate details of the event that mattered, but some broad, underlying issue which could be emphasized and highlighted by a parable, a fable, or a vivid presentation in highly figurative language" (Thompson, 17). But these are historical events that literally transpired in time and on earth.

Framework advocate Mark Ross confesses that "as adherents of the Framework Hypothesis have come from divergent theological persuasions, including some who do reject the historical character of the Genesis narrative, this suspicion seems to be confirmed. Given this diversity, it is easy for confusion to arise over just what the Framework Hypothesis is claiming and what it is denying" (Ross, 114).[40]

Blocher chastises adherents to the traditional exegesis of Genesis, in that "to talk about the alternative as 'evolution or creation', as though they were two concepts of the same order, is an unfortunate beginning. Nothing in the idea of creation excludes the use of an evolutionary procedure. Why must we tie God to one single method of action?" (Blocher, 226). He continues in the next paragraph: "If the unmodified concept of God's

---

[39] Thompson's work is clearly a Framework analysis: "the scheme was, after all, literary and artistic, not chronological and scientific." Thompson, 20. Irons lists him as a Framework advocate (Irons, 81), as does Blocher (Blocher, 50).

[40] In footnote 3 on this page Ross comments of his convictions: "My views have principally derived from the early work of Meredith G. Kline."

creative action does not exclude evolution, what are we to say about the teaching of Genesis? At this point our study again requires that we question anti-scientism. A reading which respects the forms of the language of Genesis can find no clear indication in the text for or against transformism,[41] except in the case of the creation of mankind in his unique position . . . . Thus it is at least incautious to reject the idea of an evolving creation *a priori*. There is, of course, no suggestion that the Bible positively supports an evolutionary model. The question is whether it does or does not leave the method of creation and the time scale of creation much more open than anti-scientism claims" (Blocher, 227). Consequently, the Framework Hypothesis by necessity is open to evolution, even if our brothers in presbytery are closed to it.

Furthermore, Blocher designates Bernard Ramm as a Framework advocate, and according to our agreed upon definition cited above, he meets the requirements.[42] Ramm holds that Genesis 1 provides us an artistic expression rather than an historical sequence, for "in *art* the pattern is from unformed materials to artistic creation" (Ramm, 113).[43] Of the six days of Genesis, he observes that it is "apparent that the six days are *topically* ordered or *logically* ordered, not only *chronologically* ordered" (p. 221). "The order of this communication is partially a topical arrangement" (p. 223). "The days are means of communicating to man the great fact that *God is creator*, and that *He is Creator of all*" (p. 222). This last assertion is virtually identical to the conclusions of Blocher and Thompson as cited above in this section.

Ramm is a progressive creationist, allowing for a fiat-punctuated evolution of living organisms, which "pushes" the evolutionary process over natural roadblocks imposed by the limits of natural variation: *'We believe that the fundamental pattern of creation is progressive creation. . . . Progressive creationism tries to avoid the arbitrariness of fiat creationism*

---

[41] This is Blocher's term for upward evolutionary development of biotic systems to higher forms. It allows him to urge an evolution-like transformation over time without employing the weighted term "evolution."

[42] Blocher, 50. Irons states regarding the Framework definition: "I would argue that anyone who holds to a position that meets these two criteria holds to the framework interpretation" (Irons, 3).

[43] The following parenthetical pagination points to Ramm's work.

and preserve its doctrine of the transcendence of God in creation; and it has tried to avoid the uniformitarianism of theistic evolution and preserve its sense of progress or development" (p. 113). His view holds, in part, that "the movement in Nature comes from the law of cosmical evolution which is the principle of continuity" (p. 115).

Waltke distinguishes the creation of man from that of animal by noting that "the vegetation sprang from the earth, the sea creatures originated out of the sea, and the beasts likewise trace their origin back to the earth. All these were created through the mediacy of other agents. But *not* man" (Waltke, 5:33).[44]   This must involve some form of theistic evolution or progressive creationism, which is evolution with God starring (anthropomorphically speaking, of course!) as the *deus ex machina*.

Thompson is expressly open to evolutionary theory: "As far as the Bible is concerned, it has the broad view that God is the 'Ground' of all nature. He was at its beginning, He will be at its end. He is both *above* nature, and *in* nature. That is, if you like an all-embracing theory. But it can never be proved wrong. Whatever the scientist discovers about God's world can be accommodated to such a concept" (Thompson, 14). Speaking of the creation process: "Was it by the separate instantaneous creation of each and every creature? Or was it by some process which, in the case of living things, began with some simple organism and arrived finally under the hand of God at the completed product, that is by some evolutionary process? In my view, the narrative in Genesis 1 yields no information about the divine method, only that, whatever the method, it was divine, so that any concept of a purely naturalistic evolution without God is ruled out. But there are alternatives to the two extreme positions of fiat creationism and naturalistic evolution, and men of deep Christian conviction can be found who hold such intermediate positions as *theistic evolution* or *progressive creationism*" (Thompson, 20). Here we could also rehearse Thompson's statements cited previously, urging that we "must allow for diversity of opinion among Christians" over how man was created by God (Thompson, 21).

Our concerns with the Framework Hypothesis appear to be well justified. Thompson urges our tolerant acceptance of men who hold some forms of evolution: "There are alternatives to the two extreme positions of fiat creationism [i.e., the traditional, six day creation approach] and

---

[44]This perspective fits within the vaguely announced scheme of Kline as cited previously.

naturalistic evolution, and men of deep Christian conviction can be found who hold such intermediate positions as *theistic evolution* or *progressive creationism*" (Thompson, 20).

Even the beloved and stalwart defender of the faith, J. Gresham Machen, sounded an uncertain trumpet on this matter (though he was not a Framework Hypothesis advocate, and was probably a Day Age Theorist). Reformed church historian David Calhoun cites from and comments on Machen's lectures:

> Despite his reluctance to be drawn into the debate over evolution, Machen did accept the possibility of a providentially guided evolution "as God's way of working in certain spheres . . . through nature," but he insisted that the first two chapters of Genesis and the Christian doctrine of sin and the fall required the creative power of God in sharp distinction from evolution "at the origin of the present race of man." Without going deeply into the matter, Machen believed that he was following the views of Warfield and "what Princeton has stood for all through its history."[45]

Calhoun documents the tolerance of evolution by Princeton's conservative scholar Benjamin B. Warfield. In fact, the Majority Report of the presbytery Committee (rightly) stated that "B. B. Warfield . . . had a great influence upon J. Gresham Machen" (p. 16). Mathews notes that Warfield "championed biblical authority while at the same time adhering to the new wave of evolution science" (Mathews, 108). Warfield wrote:

> The upshot of the whole matter is that there is no *necessary* antagonism of Christianity to evolution, *provided that* we do not hold to too extreme a form of evolution. . . . [If] we condition the theory by allowing the constant oversight of God in the whole process, and the occasional supernatural interferences for the production of *new* beginnings by an actual output of creative force, producing something *new* . . . we may hold to the modified theory of evolution and be Christians in the ordinary orthodox sense.[46]

Calhoun, again citing Warfield, comments:

> Warfield suggested that an evolutionary development of the human body was possible, with the gulf between the physical aspects of man and those

---

[45] David B. Calhoun, *Princeton Seminary*, vol. 2 *The Majestic Testimony: 1869-1929* (Edinburgh: Banner of Truth, 1996), 360.

[46] Calhoun, *Princeton Seminary*, 2:257.

of his brutish parents bridged by "providential guidance apart from a divine intervention." Still, man became man only when God directly and supernaturally created his soul. Warfield admitted that "the very detailed account of the creation of Eve" presented a serious problem in attempting to harmonize the Bible and evolution. Except for that passage, however, Warfield told his students that he did not think there was "any general statement in the Bible or any part of the account of creation, either as given in Genesis 1 and 2 or elsewhere alluded to, that need be opposed to evolution."[47]

Irons widely misses the mark when he responds to the concerns of adherents to the confessional view of creation. He is chagrined that we often charge that "nothing in the theory" (i.e., the Framework Hypothesis) prevents "one from believing that man evolved from lower animals." I believe the theory *does* allow for the evolution of man — even though some Framework advocates deny such a doctrine. This, of course, is not my only concern. I also deny that animal species evolved from lower order creatures, a position upon which most published Framework Hypothesis proponents are strangely silent (e.g., Kline, Blocher, and Thompson). Irons makes the incredible and mistaken counter-claim against the literal approach to Genesis: "There is nothing in the literal interpretation that deals directly with this issue either" (Irons, 72). How in the world (I ask this very literally!) could a system that claims animals were created early on Day 6 and man a few hours thereafter *on the same literal day* allow for evolutionary development from those animals into man or even between animal "kinds"? The very nature of the system forbids such!

Ecclesiastical Concerns

The Framework Hypothesis Contradicts the Presbyterian Confessional Standards. An immediate problem that confessional Presbyterians face with the Framework Hypothesis is its contradicting the Westminster Standards.[48]

---

[47] Calhoun, *Princeton Seminary*, 2:258.

[48] The Majority Report attempts to write off this point as "regarding the nuances of a single phrase" (p. 3). This "single phrase" appears *four* times in our Confessional documents, once in the Confession, twice in the Larger Catechism, and once in the Shorter Catechism. And as we show elsewhere, this phrase is not the only Confessional contradiction with the Framework Hypothesis. See, for instance: the further Confessional critique of the Framework Hypothesis in Chapter 6 below..

The Standards clearly affirm a creation "in / within the space of six days." Despite attempts to evacuate this phrase of its temporal significance and historical meaning (further illustrating the bold nature of the interpretive methodology of Framework advocates), the statements are clear and forthright.

> It pleased God the Father, Son, and Holy Ghost, for the manifestation of the glory of His eternal power, wisdom, and goodness, in the beginning, to create, or make of nothing, the world, and all things therein whether visible or invisible, *in the space of six days*; and all very good. (WCF 4:1)

> The work of creation is that wherein God did in the beginning, by the word of his power, make of nothing the world, and all things therein, for himself, *within the space of six days*, and all very good. (LC 15)

> The reasons annexed to the fourth commandment, the more to enforce it, are taken from the equity of it, God allowing us six days of seven for our own affairs, and reserving but one for himself, in these words, Six days shalt thou labor, and do all thy work: from God's challenging a special propriety in that day, The seventh day is the sabbath of the Lord thy God: from the example of God, *who in six days made heaven and earth, the sea, and all that in them is*, and rested the seventh day: and from that blessing which God put upon that day, not only in sanctifying it to be a day for his service, but in ordaining it to be a means of blessing to us in our sanctifying it; Wherefore the Lord blessed the sabbath day, and hallowed it. (LC 120)

> The work of creation is, God's making all things of nothing, by the word of his power, *in the space of six days*, and all very good. (SC 9)

The monumental labor of David Hall, of the Presbyterian Church in America, conclusively demonstrates the Westminster divines did hold to a literal understanding of Genesis 1, thereby providing us with the original intent of the Standards. In responding to a Committee paper produced by Irons, I demonstrated the Framework advocates totally misconstrue the Westminster Standards on this matter. (That content of that paper is found in Chapter 3 in this book.)

Further problems exist for *some* Framework Hypothesis advocates — advocates who fit the definition and who are accepted as legitimate representatives by the presbytery Committee Majority. And this problem appears to be a most logical extension of the Framework approach. For instance, Blocher states regarding the Sabbath: "Certainly Genesis nowhere calls the sabbath a primeval law; as Renckens points out, 'there is no text which says explicitly that *man* was from the beginning under an obligation to observe a day of rest.' Its institution is found only from Exodus onwards" (Blocher, 39). This contradicts our Standards, as well. For in them we read:

> As it is the law of nature, that, in general, a due proportion of time be set apart for the worship of God; so, in His Word, by a positive, moral, and perpetual commandment binding all men in all ages, He has particularly appointed one day in seven, for a Sabbath, to be kept holy unto him: which, from the beginning of the world to the resurrection of Christ, was the last day of the week: and, from the resurrection of Christ, was changed into the first day of the week, which, in Scripture, is called the Lord's Day, and is to be continued to the end of the world, as the Christian Sabbath. (WCF 21:7; cp. also LC 116, 120; SC 59)

See also my study below regarding the Framework Hypothesis problem with God's creative activity being a pattern for man.

PART II
EXEGETICAL STUDIES

Chapter 2
THE TRADITIONAL INTERPRETATION OF GENESIS 1

Kenneth L. Gentry, Jr.

Survey of Exegetical Arguments

Advocates of the Framework Hypothesis sometimes hold that the days of Genesis 1 present the reader with "normal solar days." They interpret these days, however, in neither the traditional manner nor in a *prima facie* fashion, as indicated by their strong tendency to put the word "day" in quotation marks.[1] Consequently, though some Framework proponents decry such (Irons, 53), the burden of proof is on their position. After all, why would the historic (Blocher, 46), first "impression" (Ridderbos, 29) view have to shoulder the burden over against a view supported by "new" (Blocher, 53), "recently developed" (Irons, 6), and "quite complicated and hard to follow" (Irons, 12 n85) arguments? This is all the more necessary since Kline himself admits: "It also needs considerable emphasis, even among orthodox exegetes, that specific evidence is required for identifying particular elements in the early chapters of Genesis as literary figures. The semi-poetic form of Genesis 1 does not make it an exception" (Kline, "Rain," 156).

Rather than literally signifying that creation occurs "in the space of six days" (WCF 4:2; LC 15; 120; SC 9), Blocher argues: "It is possible to treat the terminology of the week as figurative language, but at that moment

---

[1] As seen, for example, in Kline's and Irons' writings. Kline, "Rain": "These may disagree as to the duration of the 'days' of Genesis 1" (146); "within the era of the 'six days'" (147); "this closed era of the 'six days' was characteristic" (147); "which terminated the era of the 'six days'" (147 n3); "originated with the 'six days'" (147 n3); "the Sabbath of the seventh 'day'" (147 n4); "the world during the 'six days' era" (148); "providence during the 'six days' accords well with the analogy of subsequent divine providence" (150 n8); "the work of the 'third day'" (151); "even if the 'days' are regarded" (152); "on the 'fourth day'" (153); "the rest of the 'seventh day'"; "the contents of 'days' one to three" (154); "the 'days' are not of equal length"; "in terms of six 'days' of work followed by a seventh 'day' of rest" (155). See also: Kline, "Space and Time": "providence was in operation during the creation 'days'" and "the sequence of the 'days' is ordered" (13); "the first three 'days' of creation" (14); "made during the 'six days' includes" (14 n33). Irons: "we will then return to the 'days' of creation" (37); "the 'days' of Gen. 1 are not literal" (37); "what do these 'days' refer to?" (45).

'day' has its ordinary meaning and with that meaning plays a figurative role" (Blocher, 45). Kline contends that "when we find that God's upper level activity of issuing creative fiats from his heavenly throne is pictured as transpiring in a week of earthly days, we readily recognize that, in keeping with the pervasive contextual pattern, this is a literary figure, an earthly, lower register time metaphor for an upper register, heavenly reality" (Kline, "Space and Time," 7). Irons agrees, proposing that the days of Genesis "are part of an extended metaphor that functions as a literary framework for the creation narrative" (Irons, 3). And, of course, the Majority Report of the OPC presbytery Committee affirmed this approach (Majority Report, 8, 9).

Nevertheless, we believe that the historical understanding of the days of creation as actual calendrical time coordinates covering a temporal "space of six days" is not only the first impression one receives from the passage, but the proper exegetical conclusion. In Chapter 3 I will expose some of the logical fallacies and exegetical errors forming the foundation stones of the Framework Hypothesis. But here in the present Chapter I will survey the exegetical argument for interpreting the days of Genesis 1 in a straightforward manner that demands both their chronological succession and 24-hour duration; then we will briefly respond to certain objections charged against this exegesis.

The very historical character and foundational necessity of Genesis 1, not only to the Book of Genesis but to all of Scripture, compels us to adopt the literal nature of the six days. In fact, the chronological progression of the days provides a logical sequence (except perhaps for Day 4 to which we will return later): The days progress from creating the foundational structure for the biosphere as a habitat for life (Days 1, 2, 3, 4) to the formation of living things within that realm (Days 3b, 5, 6). It moves from the creation of *immobile* aspects of creation (Days 1-3) to the *mobile* features of creation (Days 4-6).

Argument from Primary Meaning

The preponderant usage of the word "day" (יוֹם, *yom*) in the Old Testament is of the well-known diurnal period. The overwhelming majority of its 2,304 appearances in the Old Testament clearly refer either to a normal, full day-and-night cycle, or to the lighted portion of that cycle. And both of these directly related options would be easily understood without any difficulty by the casual reader both in antiquity and today.[2] In fact, on Day 1 God himself "called" the light "day" (Ge 1:5), establishing the commonly understood, temporal significance of the term in the creation week. The daylight hours being the most important portion of the day (in that it is the time of man's productive labors, normal travel, and so forth[3]), the designation "day" can apply to the full cycle that brings the daylight back around.

Interestingly, the Mishnah refers to the creation days as literal: "The one day spoken of in the law 'It and its young' means the day together with the night that went before. This was expounded by Simeon b. Zoma: In the story of Creation it is written 'one day'; and in the law of 'It and its young' it is written, 'one day': as the 'one day' spoken of in the story of Creation means the daytime together with the night that went before" (Hullin 5:5). Josephus does, as well: "Accordingly Moses says, That in just six days the world, and all that is therein, was made" (*Ant.* 1:1).

As Berkhof declares in defending the historic exegesis of a six day creation: "In its primary meaning the word *yom* denotes a natural day; and it is a good rule in exegesis, not to depart from the primary meaning of a word, unless this is required by the context" (Berkhof, 154). Dabney points out that: "The narrative seems historical, and not symbolical; and hence the strong initial presumption is, that all its parts are to be taken in their obvious sense. . . . It is freely admitted that the word day is often used in the Greek Scriptures as well as the Hebrew (as in our common speech) for an epoch, a season, a time. But yet, this use is confessedly derivative. The natural day is its literal and primary meaning. Now, it is apprehended that in construing any document, while we are ready to adopt, at the demand of the context, the derived or tropical meaning, we revert to the primary one, when no such demand exists in the context" (Dabney, 254-55).

---

[2] "As in most languages, this basic meaning broadens to 'day (of 24 hours).'" Ernst Jenni and Claus Westermann, *Theological Lexicon of the Old Testament,* trans. Mark E. Biddle, vol. 2 (Peabody, Mass.: Hendrickson, 1997), 528. "As in other Semitic and Indo-European languages, 'day' is understood both in contrast to 'night' and as a term including both daytime and nighttime." W. von Soden, in G. Johannes Botterweck and Helmer Ringgren, eds., *Theological Dictionary of the Old Testament* (Grand Rapids: Eerdmans, 1990), 6:6.

[3] Jdg 19:9, 11; Neh 4:22; Ps 104:23; Lk 21:37; Jn 9:4; Ro 13:12; 1Th 5:5-7

Why would Moses employ a temporal term ("day") in an (allegedly) anthropomorphic context (Ridderbos, 30; Kline, "Space and Time," 14, n24; Majority Report, 8-9) — in that there is no point of contact with the eternal realm? The use of this mundane term in this (supposedly) highly stylized and sophisticated passage would generate unnecessary trouble for Moses' readers who are supposed to think of "upper register realities" (Irons, 37). For they know their God inhabits eternity and cannot be measured by days — as per Moses' own Psalm 90 (vv. 2, 4): "From everlasting to everlasting, Thou art God. . . . For a thousand years in Thy sight are like yesterday when it passes by."

This periodical time measurement was established directly by God on the first day of creation to lock in the *temporal pattern* for all earth history (Jer 33:20, 25; cp. Ge 8:22; Ps 74:16-17; Jer 31:35). "The two divisions of time known to us as Day and Night are precisely the same as those that God established at the time of creation, the *light* being the Day, and the *darkness* the Night" (Cassuto, 27). But it also provides the *temporal measure of God's creative activity* as a pattern for man's work week. Calvin explains: "God himself took the space of six days, for the purpose of accommodating his works to the capacity of men." And: "I have said above, that six days were employed in the formation of the world; not that God, to whom one moment is as a thousand years, had need of this succession of time, but that he might engage us in the consideration of his works. He had the same end in view in the appointment of his own *rest*, for he set apart a day selected out of the remainder for this special use."[4] I will have more to say about this later.

Argument from Explicit Qualification

So that we not miss his point, Moses relentlessly qualifies each of the six creation days by the phrase "evening and morning." Although the exact expression "evening and morning" only occurs in Genesis 1, outside this chapter the words "evening" and "morning" appear together in singular

---

[4] John Calvin, *Commentaries of the First Book of Moses Called Genesis*, trans. John King (Grand Rapids: Eerdmans, 1948), 1:78 (at Ge 1:5), 107 (at Ge 2:3).

statements thirty times in the Old Testament.[5] In those passages the terms are either presenting the two elements marking off a 24-hour day or speaking of the opening and closing limits of the daylight portion of a normal day. Here in Genesis 1 it seems most likely that both terms ("evening" / "morning") stand *pars pro toto*: as a part for the whole, i.e., the evening representing the whole period of darkness and the morning the whole time of light.

Of course, in the first three days of the creation week there is no "*sun-rise*" such as effects our morning. But the same phenomenon associated with our present-day sunrise (i.e., "morning") is caused by the direct, supernatural recurring pattern of light. The Hebrew word בקר (*boqer*) derives from a root that means "to break, cleave, divide," and speaks of "the breaking through of the daylight."[6] Hence, even today we may call the morning "day-*break*." The "breaking" of night's dark veil, or the "scattering" of the darkness occurs at each morning, or each new day of the creation week. This prevails even on the first three days *before* the creation of the sun. As the *Theological Dictionary of the Old Testament* observes: "Light (→ אור '*ôr*) as such is not identical with the sun (cf. Gen. 1:3f.), though it emanates from the sun."[7] The same sort of analysis holds true for the "evening" (עֶרֶב *ereb*), as well. The verbal form (עָרַב, *arab*) means "to grow dark,"[8] and is related to the noun עֹרֵב (*oreb*) which means "raven, crow" (because the verb origin means "be black").[9]

Dabney argues that this evidence alone should compel adoption of a literal day view: "The sacred writer seems to shut us up to the literal

---

[5] Ge 49:27; Ex 16:8, 13; 18:13-14; 27:21; Lev 6:20; 24:3; Nu 9:15, 21; De 16:4; 28:67; 1Sa 17:16; 1Ki 17:6; 2Ki 16:15; 1Ch 16:40; 23:30; 2Ch 2:4; 13:11; 31:3; Ezr 3:3; Est 2:14; Job 4:20; Ps 55:17; 90:6; Ecc 11:6; Isa 5:11; 17:14; Eze 24:18; 33:22; Zep 3:3.

[6] R. Laird Harris, Gleason L. Archer, Jr., and Bruce K. Waltke, eds., *Theological Wordbook of the Old Testament* (Chicago: Moody, 1980), 1:125. See also: Gerhard Kittel, ed., *Theological Dictionary of the Old Testament*, trans. by Geoffrey W. Bromiley (Grand Rapids: Eerdmans, 1964), 2:219.

[7] *Theological Dictionary of the Old Testament*, 2:223.

[8] *Theological Wordbook of the Old Testament*, 2:694.

[9] Francis Brown, S. R. Driver, C. A. Briggs, *Hebrew and English Lexicon of the Old Testament* (Oxford: Clarendon, 1972), 788.

interpretation, by describing the day as composed of its natural parts, 'morning and evening. . . .' It is hard to see what a writer can mean, by naming evening and morning as making a first, or a second 'day'; except that he meant us to understand that time which includes just one of each of these successive epochs: — one beginning of night, and one beginning of day. These gentlemen cannot construe the expression at all. The plain reader has no trouble with it. When we have had one evening and one morning, we know we have just one civic day; for the intervening hours have made just that time" (Dabney, 255; cf. Keil and Delitzsch, 50-52; Berkhof, 154; Shaw, 206[10]).

With the evening ending each day of creative activity, the following morning serves as the border separating the previous day from the next, thus introducing a new day. This passing of literal days may also be expressed as "morning after morning" (Isa 28:19). "Whenever clear reference is made to the relationship between a given day and the next, it is precisely sunrise that is accounted the beginning of the second day" (Cassuto, 28; cp. Shaw, 206; Keil and Delitzsch, 50-52).[11] In the New Testament a related pattern of "night and day" shows a full 24-hour day (Ac 20:31; 26:7; 1Th 2:9; 3:10; 2 Th 3:8; 1Ti 5:5; 2Ti 1:3). Even the presbytery Majority Report agreed with this function of "morning" (Majority Report, 5).

Mornings and evenings are phenomena recurring in the temporal realm and have no correspondence to eternity where there is neither day nor night (Rev 21:25), where time has no effect (Ps 90:4; 2Pe 3:8). "God's eternity is no indefinitely extended time, but something essentially different, of which we can form no conception. His is a timeless existence, and eternal presence" (Berkhof, 130).

If the "days" themselves are metaphorical devices, why does Moses employ this additional verbiage ("evening and morning") that gives the clear and distinct impression he wants to "lock in" their literal reality? This is especially problematic in that such delimiters would serve to confirm the (supposedly) erroneous conclusion that he is speaking of a literal six day

---

[10] See also: Reymond, *Systematic Theology*, 393; and Gerhard F. Hasel, "The 'Days' of Creation," *Origins* 21:1 (1984), 28.

[11] R. Laird Harris, Gleason L. Archer, Jr., and Bruce K. Waltke, eds., *Theological Wordbook of the Old Testament* (Chicago: Moody, 1980), 2:694.

time-frame for the duration of the creation period. The phrase "evening and morning"— which is, in fact, missing from one of the days (Day 7) and from the references to the "six days" elsewhere (Ex 20:12; 31:17) — would not be necessary for his supposed metaphorical imagery. Interestingly, in another context Irons argues that the WCF 4:2 does not teach a temporal period of six solar days because the divines did not qualify their "days" as "24-hour" days or "solar" days (Irons, 4). Why does he not follow his own line of reasoning here, noting that Moses *does* qualify his days thereby signifying their 24-hour duration?

Argument from Numerical Prefix

Genesis attaches a numeral to each of the days of creation week (1:5, 8, 13, 19, 23, 31; 2:2-3): the cardinal prefix, "one" (1:5) and ordinal prefixes on the remaining days, "second," "third," "fourth," "fifth," "sixth," and "seventh." Moses affixes numerical adjectives to *yom* 119 times in his writings. And these always signify literal days. The same holds true for the 357 times numerical adjectives qualify *yom* outside the Pentateuch.[12]

Note the following examples from Moses' writings:

•Exodus 12:15: "Seven days you shall eat unleavened bread. On the *first day* you shall remove leaven from your houses. For whoever eats leavened bread from the *first day* until the *seventh day*, that person shall be cut off from Israel."

•Exodus 24:16: "Now the glory of the LORD rested on Mount Sinai, and the cloud covered it six days. And on the *seventh day* He called to Moses out of the midst of the cloud."

•Leviticus 12:3: "And on the *eighth day* the flesh of his foreskin shall be circumcised."

---

[12] Hos 6:2 is no counter example. There the "third day" either: (1) Functions idiomatically, indicating the certainty of Israel's national resurrection, by using the literal time period at which a body begins to decompose (Jn 11:39) to underscore their hope. C. F. Keil and Franz Delitzsch, *Commentary on the Old Testament*, vol. 10, *Minor Prophets* (Grand Rapids: Eerdmans, rep. 1975), 95. Or: (2), like many of the church fathers supposed, it may allude to Christ's resurrection on the third day as containing Israel's ultimate hope. Hosea 6:2 appears to be the only backdrop for Paul's statement in 1 Cor 15:4, where he declares that Christ was raised on the third day "according to the Scriptures."

In fact, the anarthrous cardinal "one" (Heb., אֶחָד *'echad*), according to Waltke and O'Connor expresses "an emphatic, counting force."[13] Moses intends for the series of enumerated days to count off the passage of time during creation week.

As Gerhard Hasel observes: "This triple interlocking connection of singular usage, joined by a numeral, and the temporal definition of 'evening and morning,' keeps the creation 'day' the same throughout the creation account. It also reveals that time is conceived as linear and events occur within it successively. To depart from the numerical, consecutive linkage and the 'evening-morning' boundaries in such direct language would mean to take extreme liberty with the plain and direct meaning of the Hebrew language"[14] The *Theological Wordbook of the Old Testament* agrees on the linear significance of the Genesis record over against Ancient Near Eastern cyclical tendencies: "Genesis 1 betrays a totally different notion about time. Here time is conceived as linear and events occur successively within it."[15]

Argument from Numbered Series

A related, though slightly different observation to the preceding one regarding numerical prefix, notes that when *yom* appears in *sequentially numbered series* it always specifies natural days (e.g., Ex 12:15-16; 24:16; Lev 23:39; Nu 7:12-36; 29:17ff). This is another means by which Moses indicates literal days are in view, not images like "the day of the Lord" or metaphorical time frames.

By all appearance, and following upon an ever deepening tide of evidence, Genesis 1 presents a series of consecutively numbered days for a reason: to indicate sequentially flowing calendrical days, as is Moses' consistent writing practice.[16] If the days were simply structuring devices for

---

[13] Bruce K. Waltke and M. O'Connor, *An Introduction to Biblical Hebrew Syntax* (Winona Lake, Ind.: Eisenbrauns, 1990), 270.

[14] Hasel, "The 'Days' of Creation," 26.

[15] *Theological Wordbook of the Old Testament* (Chicago: Moody, 1980), 1:371.

[16] In addition, Cassuto makes an important grammatical observation based on the syntactical structure of at least one portion of the passage (on Day One): "It is a fundamental rule of Biblical narrative style that verbs describing acts that took place in sequence should

presenting us with metaphorical pictures of an orderly creation, why are they numbered? Seriatim numbering not only gives the appearance of sequential development (which the Framework Hypothesis denies for Genesis 1) but it also fits the numbering pattern of literal earthly day references elsewhere. It seems that Moses is going out of his way either to make it difficult for the reader to get his point (if he is interested only in literary effect, as per the Framework Hypothesis), or that he is locking in his meaning with various qualifying factors (if he is promoting historical accuracy, as per the traditional view).

This is all the more problematic in that the Framework Hypothesis denies temporal sequence by collapsing Days 1 and 4 into one creative episode (a serious problem with other negative implications to which we will return later; see: "Triad Symmetry Chronology" below in this section, and the Appendix). Futato argues: "The account of God's work on Days 1 and 4 are two different perspectives on the same creative work" (Futato, 16). He then cites Kline: "These effects which are said to result from the production and positioning of the luminaries on day four are the same effects that are already attributed to the creative activity of day one (Gen 1:3-5)" (Kline, "Space and Time," 7-8). If the week is anthropomorphically arranged, why this recapitulation? Men do not recapitulate work during the week.

As Young observes over against the Framework view: "If Moses had intended to teach a non-chronological view of the days, it is indeed strange that he went out of his way, as it were, to emphasize chronology and sequence. . . . It is questionable whether serious exegesis of Genesis one would in itself lead anyone to adopt a non-chronological view of the days for the simple reason that everything in the text militates against it" (Young, 100). Kidner agrees: "The march of the days is too majestic a progress to carry no implication of ordered sequence; it also seems over-subtle to adopt a view of the passage which discounts one of the primary impressions it makes on the ordinary reader" (Kidner, 54-55). Grudem concurs: "The implication of chronological sequence in the narrative is almost inescapable."[17]

---

head their respective clauses" (Cassuto, 27).

[17] Grudem, *Systematic Theology*, 303.

In fact, this chronological sequencing is further demanded by the irregular appearance of the divine appreciation formula ("it was good"). In addition to marring the "artistry" of Genesis 1,[18] we must note that *after* God creates the light, but *before* he separates it from the darkness, we read: "and God saw that the *light* was good" (Ge 1:4). On other days (but *not* at all on Day 2) the appreciation formula follows the *completed* divine activity. Why this difference? The answer points to the necessity of sequential divine activity. Note the following:

Although the creation of man as male and female is "good" — actually "very good" (Ge 1:31)—, this was not originally so. Genesis 2 informs us that at the moment when God first created man "it was *not good* for the man to be alone" (Ge 2:18). How does he correct this deficiency so that he may indeed declare man's creation "good"? He *separates* woman out of the man (Ge 2:21-22). *Then* once they *both* exist, he declares the result "good" (Ge 1:27, 31). The creation of man is not complete, is not "good," until Eve is separated out of Adam later on Day 6. The Lord is then finished with his creation of mankind, establishing male and female as the categories to prevail throughout history. This leads to the next step in our argument.

When God separates the waters below from the waters above on Day 2, absolutely *no* appreciation formula appears (see: 1:6-8). This is no accident[19] ; nor is it insignificant. Though God divides the water by creating the "firmament" which separates the waters into lower and upper realms on Day 2, he is not finished with the waters until Day 3. Then he separates the land and the water, forming what he only then calls "the Seas" (1:9-10). Then, and only then, does he declare his work with the water "good" (1:10) — which declaration interrupts the activity of Day 3 and causes the appreciation formula to appear twice on that day (1:12). Day 3 *must* follow sequentially from Day 2. The Lord is through with the waters on Day 3; they are fixed into the categories that will prevail throughout history.

And now *why* does the appreciation formula appear "out of place"? Because, like the other separations (in man, among the waters) the

---

[18] The appreciation formula appears in the middle of the creative activity on Day 1; does not appear at all on Days 2 or 7; appears *after* the creative activity on Days 3-6; appears twice on Day 3; and appears in two different styles of expression (cp. Day 1: "he saw that the light was good" and Days 3-6: "saw that it was good").

[19] The Septuagint wrongly "fixes" this deficiency by placing the formula in verse 8.

separating of light and darkness does not reach its final, permanent, providential form until later — in this case, on Day 4 when the Lord creates the heavenly bodies "to govern the day and the night, and to separate the light from the darkness" (1:18a-b). Then, and only then, is God's separating the day from the night declared "good": "and God saw that it was good" (1:18c). Irons stumbles when he writes: "Apparently the separation had already been accomplished on day one, and it must have been sufficient enough for God to declare it to be 'good'" (Irons, 25). He totally misreads the passage.

Thus, the rationale for withholding the divine appreciation formula from the separating of light and darkness, day and night, on Day 1 is because the *final, providential means of separating light and dark does not prevail until the creation and appointment of the sun, moon, and stars for that purpose* — later on Day 4. As Kline states of the divine appreciation formula: "In so far as they furthered that purpose [i.e., "to be man's habitation"] various developments were called *good*" (Kline, "Genesis," 82). We agree with his developmental observation; and that supports our sequential approach.

Irons admits: "the divine author has not only numbered the days, *a fact which by itself would lead to a sequential reading*" (Irons, 7). The sequencing of the days in seriatim fashion fits perfectly with the chronological view of the days as proposed by the *prima facie* reading of the passage, the historically accepted exegesis, and the confessional declaration — though it goes contrary to the innovative requirements of the Framework Hypothesis. The "disruption" of the artistic balance does not present us with an interesting symmetric "dissonance" (Van Gemeren, 45); it demands a chronological explanation.

Argument from Coherent Usage

The word *yom* in Genesis 1 also defines Days 4-6 — *after* God creates the sun expressly for undertaking the ongoing, providential task of marking off days (Ge 1:14, 18). Interestingly, Moses even *emphasizes* Day 4 by allocating the second greatest number of words to describe the divine activity of that day (Day 6, the climax of the creation process, generates the largest volume of words). Surely Day 4 and the following two days of creative activity are normal days — even actual *solar*-governed days. How could Moses inform his audience of the sun's creation for the expressly stated purpose of governing the day/night pattern, call this a "day," and *not* expect that his readership would also assume Days 4 through 6 are real, historical days?

In fact, nothing in the text suggests a change of temporal function for *yom* at Day 4. Moses employs a coherent usage of his expressions, maintaining his set pattern while allowing a smooth flow of temporal process from the first three days into the last three days. The first three days are measured by the very same common, temporal designator (*yom*), along with the same qualifiers ("evening and morning" boundaries, numerical prefixes, and numbered series placement). Should not Days 1-3, then, demarcate 24-hour days also? Though the sun itself does not exist on Day 1, the supernaturally-created, regularly-sequenced light does. And the sun is specifically designed to take over the lighting activity on Day 4. (For more on the "problem" of Day 4, see below.)

Once again, we see the coherence of Moses' revelation. A consistency which points to a pattern of six sequential, 24-hour days within earth history.

Argument from Divine Exemplar

The Scripture specifically patterns man's work week after God's own original creation week.

> •For in six days the LORD made the heavens and the earth, the sea, and all that is in them, and rested the seventh day. Therefore the LORD blessed the Sabbath day and hallowed it. (Ex 20:11)

> •Work shall be done for six days, but the seventh is the Sabbath of rest, holy to the LORD. . . . It is a sign between Me and the children of Israel forever; for in six days the LORD made the heavens and the earth, and on the seventh day He rested and was refreshed. (Ex 31:15-17)

Dabney's comments are helpful: "In Gen. ii:2,3; Exod. xx:11, God's creating the world and its creatures in six days, and resting the seventh, is given as the ground of His sanctifying the Sabbath day. The latter is the natural day; why not the former? The evasions from this seem peculiarly weak" (Dabney, 255). Calvin, Berkhof, Young, Kelly, Weeks, and Reymond agree.[20]

And as stated in these passages, such is not for purposes of analogy, as per the presbytery Majority Report (p. 7), but *imitation*. The Fourth Commandment clearly provides the reason that man shall work for six days and rest one day: *"For [ki, יִּכ]* in six days" the Lord created all things, then rested (Ex 20:11). Josephus writes: "Accordingly Moses says, That in just six days the world, and all that is therein, was made. And that the seventh day was a rest, and a release from the labor of such operations; whence it is that we Celebrate a rest from our labors on that day, and call it the Sabbath, which word denotes rest in the Hebrew tongue" (*Ant.* 1:1). Calvin agrees: "I have said above, that six days were employed in the formation of the world; not that God, to whom one moment is as a thousand years, had need of this succession of time, but that he might engage us in the consideration of his works. He had the same end in view in the appointment of his own *rest*, for he set apart a day selected out of the remainder for this special use."[21]

Consequently, man's work week is *subsequent* to God's original creative week, as our confessional standards note: "Q. What are the reasons annexed to the fourth commandment? A. The reasons annexed to the fourth commandment are, God's allowing us six days of the week for our own employments, his challenging a special propriety in the seventh, *his own example*, and his blessing the sabbath day" (SC 62; cp. LC 120). To make Genesis 1 a mere literary framework inverts divine revelation and denies historical reality, for man's week then becomes a pattern for God's! As Young, following G. C. Aalders, remarks: "Man is to 'remember' the Sabbath day, for God has instituted it. . . . The human week derives validity and significance from the creative week. The fourth commandment constitutes a decisive argument against any non-chronological scheme of the six days of Genesis one" (Young, 78-79; cf. Weeks, 112). Fretheim argues incisively that the Fourth Commandment is "stated in terms of the imitation of God or a divine precedent that is to be followed: God worked

---

[20] Calvin, 78; Berkhof, 155; Young, 45-47; Weeks, 115; Kelly, 109; Reymond, *A New Systematic Theology of the Christian Faith*, 395.

[21] John Calvin, *Commentaries of the First Book of Moses Called Genesis*, trans. John King (Grand Rapids: Eerdmans, 1948), 1:78 (at Ge 1:5), 107 (at Ge 2:3).

for six days and rested on the seventh, and therefore you should do the same," and that such a command is *not* for the purpose of analogy.[22] If God did not create "in the space of six days" followed by a day of rest establishing a seven day week, we have no reason for Israel's work week — for Israel employed a six day work week followed by the day of rest *before* Genesis was written.

Interestingly, Framework proponent Wenham comments: "Exod 16:22-30 suggests that Israel first learned about the Sabbath in the wilderness, though Exod 20:8, like this passage [Ge 2:2-3], asserts that the Sabbath idea is as old as creation itself. It observing the seventh day as holy, man is imitating his creator's example" (Wenham, 36).

Kline notes that "earthly time is articulated in the astronomical phenomena that structure its flow" (Kline, "Space and Time," 7). That is true for days, months, and years — but not for a *week*. The calendrical week is rooted in historical, not astronomical, reality, that is, in God's original creative activity, just as Exodus 20:11 and 31:15-17 inform us.

God dwells in timeless eternity (Isa 57:15) where there is no succession of moments or temporal constraints (2Pe 3:8). Consequently, to what could the creation days be analogous? Irons states that: "God has not chosen to reveal that information" (Irons, 66). But as Pipa complains: "then the analogy is useless" (Pipa, 172). Nor may we suggest that the days are anthropomorphic days (as per Majority Report, 8-9; Irons, 67-68; Blocher, 50-57), for anthropomorphic language "can be applied to God alone and cannot properly be used of the six days" (Young, 58).

I will return to the sabbath question again in Chapter 3.

Argument from Plural Expression

Exodus 20:11 and 31:17 also teach that God created the heavens and the earth "in six *days*" (mYm!y* / yammim). As Reymond reminds us: "Ages are never expressed by the word *yammim*."[23] In fact, the plural *yammim*

---

[22] Terence E. Fretheim, "Were the Days of Creation Twenty-Four Hours Long?" in *The Genesis Debate: Persistent Questions About Creation and the Flood*, ed. Ronald R. Youngblood (Nashville: Nelson, 1986), 20.

[23] *A New Systematic Theology of the Christian Faith*, 394.

occurs 858 times in the Old Testament, and always refers to normal days. Exodus 20:11 (like Ge 1) lacks any kind of poetic structure; it presents a factual, historical accounting. By this shorthand statement, God sums up his creative activity in a way that not only comports with, but actually demands a six day creative process.

Interestingly, Exodus 20:11 lacks the preposition ב (*b*). Thus, God's working six days is expressed by means of the accusative of temporal determination, "a usage that indicates how long an action took . . . . That is, 'during six days God made the heavens and the earth.' This use implies both that the days were normal days, and that the days were contiguous" (Shaw, 217).[24]

Argument from Unusual Statement

Due to the Jewish practice of reckoning days from evening to evening, the temporal pattern "evening and morning" may seem unusual (because it assumes the day began in the morning, passes into evening, and closes at the next morning). Cassuto explains for us that "whenever clear reference is made to the relationship between a given day and the next, it is precisely sunrise that is accounted the beginning of the second day" (Cassuto, 28; cp. Hamilton, 121; Kidner, 47). For example, Exodus 12:18 has the fourteenth evening at the conclusion of the fourteenth day (cp. Lev 23:32).

Therefore, Genesis 1 presents literal days reckoned according to the civil — non-ritual, non-symbolic — pattern. We see evening closing the daylight time, followed by morning which closes the darkness, thereby beginning a new day (e.g., Gen 19:33-34; Ex 10:13; 2Sa 2:32). Again, this all dovetails nicely with the traditional and confessional interpretation of a creation "in the space of six days" over against the literary view of an open-ended creation time-frame consuming billions of years (cf. Kline, "Space and Time," 1).

Argument from Alternative Idiom

Had Moses intended that six days represent six eras, he could have chosen a less confusing and more fitting expression: עוֹלָם (*olam*). This

---

[24] See Paul Joüon, *A Grammar of Biblical Hebrew,* tr. and rev., T. Muraoka (Rome: Pontifical Biblical Institute, 1991), Par. 126i.

word is often translated "forever," but it also means a long period of time. For instance, *olam* describes the temporal longevity (short of eternity) of the Passover (Ex. 12:24), a slave's commitment to his earthly master (Exo. 21:6), various levitical functions (Ex. 29:28; 30:21; Lev. 6:18, 22; 7:343, 36; 10:15; 16:29, 31; 17:7; 23:14, 21, 41; 24:3; Num. 18:8; etc.), and Joshua's memorial stones (Josh. 4:7).

Furthermore, Moses should not have qualified the days with "evening and morning." This, of course, is more relevant to the Day Age theory. But it serves to broaden the evidentiary basis of the traditional, literal six day view.

Argument from Scholarly Admissions

Remarkably, scholars who deny the reality of the historically accepted exegetical conclusion of a six day creation process recognize Moses actually meant literal days:

• Herman Gunkel: "The 'days' are of course days and nothing else."[25]

• Gerhard von Rad: "The seven days are unquestionably to be understood as actual days and as a unique, unrepeatable lapse of time in the world."[26]

• John Skinner: "The interpretation of *yom* as eon is opposed to the plain sense of the passage and has no warrant in Hebrew usage."[27]

• Adolf Dillman: "The reasons advanced by ancient and modern writers for construing these days to be periods of time are inadequate."[28]

• James Barr: "If the word day in these chapters does not mean a period of twenty-four hours, the interpretation of Scripture is hopeless. So far as I know there is no professor of Hebrew or Old Testament at any world-class university who does not believe that the writers of Genesis 1-11 intended to convey to their readers that creation took place in a series of six days

---

[25] Cited in Hasel, "The 'Days' of Creation," 21.

[26] G. von Rad, *Genesis*, rev. ed., tr. J. H. Markes (Philadelphia: Westminster, 1972), 65.

[27] John Skinner, *A Critical Commentary on Genesis*, 2 ed., (Edinburgh: T and T Clark, 1930), 21.

[28] Cited in Leupold, *Genesis*, 57.

which were the same as the days of twenty-four hours we now experience."[29]

•Ernst Jenni asserts that *yom* in Genesis 1 means: "in the sense of the astronomical or calendrical unit."[30]

•Victor Hamilton: "Whoever wrote Gen. 1 believed he was talking about literal days." (Hamilton, 54)

•Gordon Wenham: "There can be little doubt that here 'day' has its basic sense of a 24-hour period. The mention of morning and evening, the enumeration of the days, and the divine rest on the seventh show that a week of divine activity is being described here." (Wenham, 19)

•Van Till: Theistic evolutionist Christian scholar Howard Van Till admits that "the days of the Genesis 1 story are clearly ordinary days."[31]

In summary: under divine inspiration while writing historical narrative, Moses informs us that God created the whole universe in the span of six chronologically successive and contiguous periods of 24-hours duration each. The evidence is overwhelming and not in the least "subtle." Nevertheless, Framework (and Day Age) advocates see problems, to which we now briefly turn.

Response to Alleged Problems

Several of these "problems" with the six day creation position are generated from within the Day Age camp, rather than the Framework Hypothesis school of interpretation. Nevertheless, I desire to demonstrate the integrity of the traditional and confessional exegesis which results in the literal, six day creation approach to Genesis 1, even as I respond to the Framework Hypothesis specifically. Later I will counter other alleged "problems" with the historically accepted view of Genesis 1 while critiquing the three-fold foundation of the Framework Hypothesis (see Chapter 3).

---

[29] Personal communication cited in Kelly, *Creation and Change*, 51.

[30] Ernst Jenni in Jenni and Westermann, *Theological Lexicon of the Old Testament*, 2:528.

[31] Howard Van Till, *The Fourth Day* (Grand Rapids: Eerdmans, 1986), 91.

The Fourth Day Problem (Gen. 1:14-19)

Objection: On Day 4 God creates the sun to "give light on the earth" (1:15) and "to separate the day from the night" (1:14). But light was previously created on Day 1 (1:3), and there "God separated the light from the darkness" (1:4). This shows that the creation days are not chronologically ordered, but thematically cross-linked. In this particular case, Day 4 is recapitulating Day 1; it is not making chronological progress over Day 1. Thompson emphasizes that this "presents serious difficulties on any chronological view" (Thompson, 20). Irons concurs, noting that "neither the day-age nor the literal reading of Gen. 1 can do justice to the close connection between day one and day four" (Irons, 25). In fact, this argument holds a special "importance as an independent argument against the solar-day and day-age views" (Kline, "Space and Time," 7).

I will specify the nature of the alleged problem Framework advocates have with the traditional exegesis. Irons provides a helpful explanation and defense of the entire Framework Hypothesis in which he provides a succinct statement of the Day 4 "problem." I will cite Irons, then critique his argument. Irons presents the following three-fold argument:

(1) Framework Hypothesis advocates complain that the traditional exegesis promotes an unnecessary supernaturalism. "Those who wish to maintain a literal, sequential reading argue that the light of day one was maintained by supernatural power (or at least some non-ordinary means) for three days, until the creation of the luminaries on day four. . . . But this interpretation is inconsistent with the principle stated in Gen. 2:5: during the creation period, God maintained the created entities by ordinary providence rather than supernatural power" (Irons, 25). Elsewhere he cites Kline's maxim "that there was an 'avoidance of unnecessary supernaturalism in providence' during the creation week" (Irons, 34; Kine, "Rain," 150).

(2) Framework Hypothesis proponents argue that the historic exposition suppresses the significance of the sun's creation. The literal interpretation "does not explain why the luminaries were said to have been created 'in order to give light on the earth . . . and to separate the light from the darkness' (1:17-18). It would be one thing if the text had said that the luminaries were created in order *to maintain* the previously created light and the previously established separation. But that is not what the text says. Rather, the luminaries were created in order *to give* light and *to separate* the light from the darkness. Exegetically there is no way around the stubborn

fact that the divine purpose for the creation of light on day one and the purpose of the creation [*sic*] the luminaries on day four are one and the same" (Irons, 25).

(3) Framework Hypothesis adherents suggest that the long accepted interpretation overlooks the integrity of the divine labor. "Furthermore, even if an exegetical case could be made for reading the two infinitives ('to separate' — 1:14, 18) as shorthand for 'to maintain the separation,' there would still be another problem. Apparently the separation had already been accomplished on day one, and it must have been sufficient enough for God to declare it to be 'good.' Why, then, does God feel the need to discard that arrangement and replace it with a new one on day four?" (Irons, 25).

Some would proffer other "problems,"[32] but Irons has nicely summarized these as the leading Framework counter-evidences against the historic, traditional, and confessional exegesis.

Response: I will interact with Irons' presentation in reverse order:

(1) Irons stumbles in his third argument by misreading the Day 1 account. He mistakenly claims "the separation" was "sufficient enough for God to declare it to be 'good.'" His error is caused not only by a superficial reading of these verses, but by failing to note the pattern of their setting. Since this has already been noted above, I will only briefly rehearse the matter here.

a.) On Day 1 God declares "good" the newly created *light* — but *not* his *separating* it from darkness to form the day/night pattern. Note that *after* God declares the newly created light "good," *then* he separates the light from the darkness (Ge 1:3-4). This unusual pattern (appreciation formula *before* completion of work) occurs for a reason: the final, providential mechanism for separating night and day (the sun, moon, and stars) will not be created until Day 4. Thus, when Day 4 ends, and the permanent historical means effecting the light/dark pattern is in place, we finally read:

---

[32] For instance, we often hear the complaint that vegetation cannot grow without the sun. But this is no problem to the traditional view: First, actually plants require *light*, and God directly creates that on the First Day. Second, even apart from this consideration, on the traditional interpretation the plants would only be denied light for a few hours — less than one day, for on Day 4 God creates the sun. Others point to the overly busy nature of Adam on the sixth day. But when asked, we realize we do not know many animals he named, and that probably they were only those in his immediate environment. Consequently, the "problem" fades away upon closer investigation.

"it was good" (Ge 1:18). This matter is widely noted by commentators.[33] For instance, Hamilton well argues:

> The major difference between this work of separation and the other two in Gen. 1 is that here the pronouncement of God's benedictional statement — *God saw how beautiful the light was* — precedes the separation. In vv. 6-8 and 14-19 this sentence of evaluation follows the separation. Thus it is the light itself that is *beautiful* (or good, Heb., *tôb*), not the creation per se of time into units of light and darkness. (Hamilton, 120).

As observed previously, this is similar to the separation of the waters above and below on Day 2, which is not declared "good" until the final separation from the land on Day 3 (Ge 1:9) (Waltke, 5:29). Waltke notes: "The sky was separated from the water on the second day, but no pronouncement of good was given because spatial separation was not yet complete. Only with the separation of land, the third life supportive system, did God pronounce the spatial separation as good or complete" (Waltke, 5:29).

Irons' mistake is no mere writer's gaffe; rather it exposes a fault line running through the Framework foundation itself. The well-ordered revelation of Genesis 1 assumes chronological progress — even here where the sequential approach is thought doomed. *Even the appreciation statements await the proper stage of progress and are not spoken too soon.*

Kline complains that creating light on Day 1 and the light-bearers on Day 4 "would raise questions about the wisdom of the divine procedure" (Kline, "Space and Time," 9). Why would God create a light source on Day 1, then create the sun for purposes of lighting on Day 4? But the final establishment of the permanent arrangement on Day 4 no more casts a shadow upon God's wisdom than does his employing separate and distinct fiats to separate the waters above and below (1:6), *then* on the next "day" the land from the waters (1:9).

Besides, this two-step procedure surely casts less doubt upon "the wisdom of the divine procedure" than does a creation over billions of years, entailing tremendous chaos and upheaval, and the arising of sentient life forms, the constant deaths of individual members, and the extinction of whole species. Especially when we realize that this demands that after such

---

[33] See: Keil and Delitzsch, 54 (n1); Cassuto 34, 40; Wenham 19; Mathews, 151; Waltke, 5:29; Sailhammer, 26; and Hamilton, 124.

a multi-billion year creation process, we have only just *very, very recently* exited that creation process — all the while expecting the any moment return of Christ to *end* the temporal order! The historical understanding of Genesis 1 greatly emphasizes the wisdom, power, and majesty of God by creating quickly and "all very good," without the trial and error destruction of whole families of sentient life forms.

b.) Most of the material in Genesis 1 *demands* chronological order. Even Framework advocates recognize this, though they write it off as "accidental" — despite the numbered series structure, and all else we have discussed (Futato, 1; Kline, 154; Irons, 59 n128; Blocher, 50). Such a context and flow suggests that even the surprising order of light-then-sun must also be chronological.

Not only is Genesis 1 structured by fifty-five waw consecutives, indicating narrative sequence, but note: Separating the waters on Day 2 requires their prior creation on Day 1 (Ge 1:2d). Creating the sea on Day 3 must predate the sea creatures of Day 5. Day 3 logically has dry land appearing before land vegetation later that day. Day 3 must also predate Day 6, in that land must precede land animals and man. In fact, Days 1-4 establish the environment of man and animal. Day 6 must appear as the last stage of creation, in that man forms the obvious climax to God's creation. Day 6 logically has man being created after animal life (Days 5 and 6) in that he is commanded to rule over the animals. Day 7 must conclude the series in that it announces the cessation of creation (Ge 2:2). And so on.

(2) Irons' second argument is widely deemed a serious complication for the traditional view by those adopting an artistic-literary approach to Genesis 1. Framework advocates argue that the luminaries are created *to give* light and *to separate* light and darkness, but that these functions are already taken care of on Day 1. The luminaries, they argue, are not to *maintain* that which already exists — they *establish* it. In addition to that which is noted above from Irons' paper, we learn from the presbytery's Majority Report that God "named the light 'Day' and the darkness 'Night' (Gen. 1:5). In naming them, he established their essential character and significance. If the characters were to change; the names would need to change as well" (Majority Report, 4). Thus, it is felt, these cannot be distinct creative events from separate creational days; Day 4 must be recapitulating Day 1.

Consider the following rejoinders.

a.) This does not seem a significant problem to many notable commentators. For one example, Hamilton notes: "What the author states is that God caused the light to shine from a source other than the sun for the first three 'days.'" In his footnote he explains: "The Bible begins and ends by describing an untarnished world that is filled with light, but no sun (cf. Rev. 22:5). Should not the one who is himself called 'light' (1 John 1:5) have at his disposal many sources by which he dispatches light into his creation? Just as Gen. 1 says there can be a day and light without sun, so Matt. 2 says there can be a son without a father. Calvin comments, 'Therefore the Lord, by the very order of creation, bears witness that he holds in his hands the light, which he is able to impart to us without the sun and moon'" (Hamilton, 121 n7). Young agrees (Young, 95).

b.) Furthermore, Scripture elsewhere suggests that light existed apart from the sun. Job 38:19a challenges: "Where is the way to the dwelling of light?" If the answer is "the sun," the question is not all that much of a contest. 2 Corinthians 4:6a declares: "For God, who said, 'Light shall shine out of darkness.'" Clearly "the language of vv. 5-6 resonates with key vocabulary used of the creation in the opening chapter of Genesis ('image of God,' 'God . . . said, 'Let there be light').[34] In fact, the Bible begins (Ge 1:3) and ends with light apart from the sun (Rev 22:5).

In addition, after surveying the evidence, Young declares: "Day four, we may assert with all confidence, presupposes the existence of the light which was created in day one" (Young, 97; cp. Sailhammer, 34). The revelation of God's creating the astral bodies on Day 4, *assumes* the chronological sequence of Genesis 1. Day 4 presupposes light/darkness and day/night already exist. On Day 1 God: (1) creates the light by direct fiat; (2) personally separates it from the darkness; then (3) calls the light "Day" and the darkness "Night" (1:5). On Day 4, though, God creates the *luminaries* (מָאוֹר, *mā'ôr*, "place of light") themselves, "to separate the day from the night" (1:14) and "the light from the darkness" (1:19).

Notice the way the "Day" and the "Night" are mentioned: the *luminaries* separate that which *already* exists (light and dark) and which produces an effect already established ("Day" and "Night"). The luminaries

---

[34] Paul Barnett, *The Second Epistle to the Corinthians* (NICNT) (Grand Rapids: Eerdmans, 1997), 225. Barnett should have begun with 2 Co 4:4, not at 4:5.

do not *initiate* the light, nor do they begin the light/dark sequencing; that was established on Day 1. The sun was created to fit the day, not vice versa. On Day 1 God created the light *de novo* and named the "Day" and the "Night"; on Day 4 he creates the "place of light," the *mā'ôr*, i.e., the "luminaries." The luminaries are "set" to take over the lighting function, to "govern" it's coming and going (Cassuto, 43). As Hamilton puts it: "The creation of light anticipates the creation of sunlight" (Hamilton, 121). Furthermore, the luminaries are placed "in the expanse of the heavens" (1:14, 17), which was not created until Day 2. And the luminaries formed on Day 4 are to "give light on the earth" (1:15), which function assumes the prior extrusion of the earth's surface from beneath the waters and its naming ("earth") on Day 3 (1:10).

The presbytery Majority Report correctly observed that naming the "Day" and the "Night" establishes "their essential character and significance" (p. 4). This is *precisely* in keeping with my previous arguments. And that is why I hold to a literal twenty-four hour day. By God's creating light then naming it's earthly appearance "Day," we learn the character of the Day that God has ordained for temporal history: It is (1) a period of time, (2) for light to shine on the earth, that (3) continually returns (4) during every twenty-four hour cycle. What is the problem? We do not see the *sun* included in the definition of "Day" here in Holy Writ, just the *light*. We know, of course, that *today* we think of the sun when we think of daylight, but in Genesis 1 we are dealing with a unique period of time: the creation of the entire universe by the very command of God. God from the very beginning established the time-structure of the created order by ordaining the cycles of light and darkness — even before creating the sun.

What is more, Meredith Kline even notes that the "heavens and earth" of Genesis 1:1 "are viewed in their earliest not perfected state, yet as a totality, this being the idiomatic force in Hebrew of such contrasted pairs" (Kline, "Genesis," 82; cp. Kline, "Glory," 250). As Wenham expresses it: "Commentators often insist that the phrase 'heaven and earth' denotes the completely ordered cosmos. Though this is usually the case, totality rather than organization is its chief thrust here. It is therefore quite feasible for a mention of an initial act of creation of the whole universe (v 1) to be followed by an account of the ordering of different parts of the universe (vv 2-31)" (Wenham, 15). Consequently, the enormous change effected from the universe's "earliest not perfected state" to their final well-ordered condition does not require calling the *earliest* stage something other than "heavens and earth." Why may not the word "day" be used before and after the sun — especially since the four fundamental characteristics of the "day" still prevail.

The Majority Report of the presbytery was quite mistaken when it alleged: "The 'Day' must be an ordinary day, governed and lighted by the sun. The 'Night' must be an ordinary night, governed and lighted by the moon and the stars. This is what those words mean. There is nothing in the text that suggests we are reading about an orderly alternation of light and darkness, supernaturally maintained in the absence of sun, moon, and stars" (p. 3).

In the first place, I have read and re-read the Mosaic revelation regarding Day 1, and I have yet to find mention of "the sun." The word "Day" (*yom*, יוֹם) does not *mean* "an ordinary day, governed and lighted by the sun." The Hebrew word for the "sun" (*shemesh*, שֶׁמֶשׁ) is not a constitute element of the word "day," which is *yom* (יוֹם). And secondly, despite the bold denial by our Framework brothers, there *is*, in fact, something "in the text that suggests we are reading about an orderly alternation of light and darkness, supernaturally maintained in the absence of sun, moon, and stars." Incredibly, *every element* of their denial is justified by reading the text of Genesis 1:3-5! Consider the text for yourself (with our interpretive comments in brackets): "Then God said, 'Let there be light' [this surely is a supernatural activity]; and there was light [this surely is a supernatural result — one that does *not* mention the sun at all]. And God saw that the light [not "the sun"] was good; and God [himself, supernaturally] separated the light from the darkness. And God called the light [just mentioned] day, and the darkness He called night. And there was evening and there was morning, one day."

The Majority Report was correct when it noted of "the man on the street" that "he would never guess from this language that what is being referred to is a sunless day" (p. 4). *But* the "man on the street" is not simply given a collection of terms — "day," "night," "morning," "evening" — to judge by. The man on the street should not be playing Scrabble, but reading a flowing text. Neither is he left to "guess" about the meaning. Rather he is given a carefully structured passage revealing six successive days which states that the naked light was created on Day 1, and *only later* on Day 4 the sun. In *that* context, he would do what the "majority" (Blocher) of Christians have done from time immemorial: Recognize that in this *unique* period, light existed three days *before* the sun. Thus once again, we must recall that Ridderbos confesses that "one who reads Genesis 1 without prepossession or suspicion is almost bound to receive the impression that the author's intent is to say that creation took place in six ordinary days" (Ridderbos, 29). Framework advocate Mark Ross agrees: "It is admitted by all that the first impression of Genesis 1:1— 2:3 is of a sequential, chronological account of a six day creation with a seventh day of rest" (Ross, 118).

Incredibly the Majority Report stated of the traditional view: "that interpretation cannot possibly derive this impression from the text of the first three days" (p. 5). That is *precisely* the *only* impression that can be derived "from the text of the first three days"! The Framework Hypothesis has to read material *back into* the text of the first three days, to make their view work. I stated that this assertion is "incredible" because after discounting the traditional interpretation that derives solely from what the text actually says, the Majority read into Genesis 1 the following anti-textual story: "The picture in Genesis 1 clear. God wakes up. He works until evening. He lies down for the night and repeats the process in the morning" (p. 8).[35] The literary approach of the Framework Hypothesis *denies* what is *expressly written* so that it may *affirm* what is *absolutely absent* from the text. To quote Irons concerns in another context: "But that is not what the text says" (Irons, 25).

Furthermore, the Majority Report argument is torn by dialectical tension in its own successive paragraphs on this point. In its fifth paragraph on page 8 it states: "More subtle, but more to the point, God's manner of working is anthropomorphic. He works during the day. He stops when it gets dark. When the sun rises He goes to work again." Notice the "more subtle" statement. The *American Heritage Dictionary* defines "subtle" as follows: "a. So slight as to be difficult to detect or analyze; elusive. b. Not

---

[35] Sadly *on this Framework analysis*, E. J. Young misses what is "clear" and what the Holy Spirit has gone "out of his way" to emphasize, when he writes of "the non-chronological view of the days" that: "everything in the text militates against it" (Young, 100).

57

immediately obvious; abstruse."[36] But then in the very next paragraph subtlety gives way to unmistakable clarity: "The picture in Genesis 1 is clear. God wakes up. He works until evening. He lies down for the night and repeats the process in the morning. The Spirit has gone out of His way to present the work of God on the analogy of the work of man." Which is it? Is this picture "subtle," i.e., difficult to detect, elusive, as per paragraph five? Or is it so "clear" that it is evident "the Spirit has gone out of His way to present" the picture, as in paragraph six? Such exaggerations and contradictions constantly mar the Framework Hypothesis.

Now back to the matter of explaining the Day 4 problem. According to Young, "the origin of heaven and earth, however, was simultaneous [cf. Ge 1:1], but the present arrangement of the universe was not constituted until the fourth day. The establishment of this arrangement is expressed by the verb וַיִּתֵּן , but we are not told how God 'gave' or 'set' these light-bearers in the firmament" (Young, 95). That is, apparently the material and rough order of the astral bodies was created on Day 1 and in "their earliest, not perfected state" (Kline, "Genesis," 82; "Glory," 250; cp. Young, 9, 14, 95), but were not finalized until later when they become the actual sun, moon, and stars that we know today. This is much like our hard rock and cool water planet being created to be our habitat (Is 45:18), though originally in its first stages it was an inundated and uninhabitable mass (1:2). Later it was properly organized by the various divine fiats effecting the two water separations, providing its atmosphere, seas, and dry land (Days 1 and 3), clothing it with verdure (Day 3), and populating with all the sentient life forms, including man (Days 5, 6). Wenham notes of Genesis 1:14: "This verse, though, affirms the relationship between sun and daylight for all time form the creation of the sun on the fourth day. It must therefore be supposed that the first three days were seen as different: then light and darkness alternated at God's behest" (Wenham, 22).

Now on Day 4 the astral bodies are transformed from dark masses to be made into light-bearers, "luminaries," localized places for light. They are not only to separate day and night and give light upon the earth (as the God-created light on Day 1 did previously), but also to serve "for signs, and for seasons, and for years" (1:14). God's directly sustaining the naked light

---

[36] *The American Heritage Dictionary of the English Language*, 3d. ed. (New York: Houghton and Mifflin, 1992).

during the first three days was not intended for an *ongoing* and *permanent* illuminatory mechanism; the original light directly ordained and briefly sustained by God set the *temporal pattern* by distinguishing the short-term night-and-day cycle during the first half of the original creation week. The final, providential mechanisms taking over that short-term cycle (the sun, moon, and stars) will also provide for measuring whole "seasons" and entire "years" for the long term, not just the original, limited seven day week.

(3) Irons' first argument, derived from Kline, is perhaps the most surprising to the traditional interpreter. And it is only a problem in the minds of Framework advocates; it is no problem for a theology of creation by an omnipotent God. Framework advocates speak of "unnecessary supernaturalism" during the creation period. But we must remember that the creation period was a unique, unrepeatable period wherein the entire universe was created *ex nihilo*. The very idea of *ex nihilo* creation presupposes its highly supernaturalistic character. The traditional exegesis is not in the least embarrassed by any charge of "unnecessary supernaturalism" — especially since nothing required is bizarre or illogical from within a Christian theistic worldview.

Rather than serving as a trampling foot crushing the traditional exegesis, Framework reliance on Genesis 2:5, to which Irons refers, is the system's Achilles' Heel,. This is true both in this particular argument as well as in the broader system-structuring. I will note a couple of quick debilitating problems here, while reserving my main response to the Genesis 2:5 argument for a more thorough critique in Chapter 3.

Observe that *even if* this lone verse highlights deficiencies at a certain stage (Day 3) in the temporal order of creation, Kline's providential argument is not the most likely solution. First, the two-fold deficit which supposedly dissuades us from an "unnecessary supernaturalism" is: no *rain* and no *man*, which together explain the problem of no vegetation. This supposedly demonstrates "that as far as the time frame is concerned, with respect to both the duration and sequence of events, the scientist is left free of biblical constraints in hypothesizing about cosmic origins" (Kline, "Space and Time," 1).

Now then, what are we to make of this "unnecessary supernaturalism" principle, as claimed by Framework advocates? Ironically, God rectifies the man-deficit by a direct, miraculous, and highly — "unnecessarily"? — supernaturalistic activity (Ge 2:7), as even Kline admits ("Genesis," 83)!

Why, then, must we require that the other problem (the rain-deficit) be handled by means of slow providence? The manner by which God creates man wrecks the "unnecessary supernaturalism" argument by importing a bold supernaturalism of the highest sort into the account. And remarkably, at the very point where slow providence is allegedly affirmed — *and* in a way that appears to the liberal to suggest the most obvious evidence that "the conception of Jehovah is extremely primitive," and that "the story, with all its naive beauty, is intended for an audience intellectually and spiritually immature."[37]

Second, *even if* rain is lacking after the land extrusion and before its vegetational cloaking, the text specifically declares that *God's divine fiat* causes the appearance of vegetation (1:11). This fiat affirmation demonstrates God's activity here is 'necessarily supernatural,' rather than merely providential.

Kline's "new" (Blocher, 53) approach to creation theology based on Genesis 2:5 is not sufficient to overthrow the long-standing traditional and confessional exegesis. It cannot turn aside the "majestic march of days" that becomes "one of the primary impressions it makes on the ordinary reader" (Kidner). Nor may it disrupt the obvious "chronological succession of events" (Young). If during the course of providence-dominated post-creation history God can impose "unnecessary supernaturalism" upon the world (as in Moses' turning a river into blood, Joshua's long day, Hezekiah's sun reversal, Jesus' quieting the mighty tempest, and so forth), why is it so remarkable that during this uniquely supernatural creation period, God would employ this one surprising and highly-supernaturalistic means of providing light for three days without the sun? Especially in that he produces light apart from the sun frequently today (e.g., lightning) (Cassuto, 26).

The literary approach to Genesis 1 from the Framework Hypothesis does not overthrow the "time honored" (Irons), "majority" (Blocher), "dominant" (Kline) exegesis of historic Christianity and of confessional reformed orthodoxy.

---

[37] Theodore H. Robinson, "Genesis," in Frederick Carle Eiselen, Edwin Lewis, and David G. Downey, *The Abingdon Bible Commentary* (New York: Abingdon, 1929), 221.

The Sabbath Day Problem (Gen. 2:2-3)

Objection: Genesis 2:2-3 establishes the seventh day of God's rest, which is ongoing and not a literal 24-hour day. The seventh day lacks the "evening/morning" qualifier, indicating that it continues today. Furthermore, the very fact that God has ceased and never resumed his creational work demands the seventh day continues. In fact, Hebrews 4:1-4 speaks of this sabbath day as the abiding rest of God. Both Day Age and Framework Hypothesis advocates bring this objection to bear against the traditional view, but in different ways.

For the Day Age theorist the ongoing nature of God's seventh day sabbath (based on Psa. 95 and Heb. 4) shows us that the preceding six days should also be long periods of time. This is especially significant in that Genesis 2:2-3 is the very context of the revelation of the six creative days and, in fact, is the concluding day of the original creation week.

Harris vigorously asserts: "I cannot see how it can be argued in the face of these verses [Psa 95 and Heb 4] that God's rest was only 24 hours." He continues: "Now if God's seventh day is an eternal day, as argued in the Psalms and Hebrews and yet it is paralleled to man's seventh day Sabbath, it follows that our weekdays cannot be duplicates of God's days of creation and rest, but are symbolic thereof. It seems to be an inescapable conclusion that our seventh day 24-hour Sabbath is symbolic of God's eternal Sabbath of rest from creation. If so, then there is no reason at all to deny that our particular six 24 hour days of labor are symbolic of, not equivalent to, God's six long days of creative labor" (Harris, 110).

For Framework advocates this day is crucial for establishing their Two Register Cosmogony. Consequently, Kline also believes this day was a long period of time (but for a different reason): "The seventh day has to do altogether with God, with the upper register" (Kline, "Space and Time," 10). Irons concurs: "God's rest 'on the seventh day' is interpreted in Hebrews as an upper register reality . . . . If the seventh day is an upper register day, then how can the previous six days be lower register days? In addition, the fact that the seventh day is *eternal* supports the notion that the entire seven-day scheme is a metaphor for the upper register time-frame of creation" (Irons, 51).

Response: Several distractions lead this battering ram of argumentation off into the wrong direction, leaving the traditional exegesis intact.

(1) The argument is an *argument from silence*. The claim that *the sabbath day of Genesis 2:2-3* is a long "day" — as argued by both Harris *and* Framework advocates — is an argument derived from outside the text. The revelation of God *in Genesis 2:2* does not inform us that *that* original sabbath day is eternal. As Keil well notes: "We must not, without further ground, introduce this true and profound idea into the seventh creation-day" (Keil and Delitzsch, 69). Indeed, such an argument rests "a great deal of weight on a very narrow and thin exegetical bridge" (Kelly, 111). The text here clearly presents the seventh day as another in the well-defined series of days within the original creation week. In fact, this "seventh day" is the *conclusion* to the creation week, not only in that it is the seventh of only seven days, all properly enumerated. But also, on that day we have the historical cessation of the divine creative activity.

Literally Genesis 2 informs us that God "*ceased*" his labor. As Wenham observes: "'He rested' שבת has three closely related senses: 'to cease to be,' 'to desist from work,' and 'to observe the sabbath.' It is clear that the second sense is central here" (Wenham, 35). Mathews adds: "The verb translated 'rested' here means 'the *cessation* of creative activity'; it has this same sense in its only other occurrence in Genesis, where God promises the postdiluvian world that the times and seasons 'will never cease' (8:22). Elsewhere we find that God 'rested' (*nûah*, Exod 20:11; *napaš*, 31:17), but here the passage speaks of the absence of work — 'he abstained' from work" (Mathews, 178; cp. Kidner, 53). Even Framework adherent Thompson admits the word in Genesis 2 means "'cease,' or 'stop'" (Thompson, 22).[38] In Genesis 2:2 Moses declares simply that God ceased his creation process. And he ceased it at a particular moment in time, i.e., on *that* particular day.[39] In fact, God does not "rest" from *all* labor, for he "made" (אָשָׂה, *asah*) coats of skins for Adam and Eve (Ge 3:21). He *does* permanently cease from creating the world, but not from *all* temporal creative activity.

---

[38] See also: Hyers, *The Meaning of Creation*, 75.

[39] Interestingly, just a few verses previous to the three-fold "rest" declaration (of Ge 2:2-3), God creates man in his "image," so that he will reflect God. Here in Genesis 2:2-3 cessation from labor is emphasized after six days of work. Man is to imitate God in this: a six day work week followed by a day of rest.

Some 1500 years after Moses wrote Genesis the writer of Hebrews refers to the original, creational sabbath in Hebrews 4:4b to *develop* the concept of an ongoing or eschatological sabbath. But his *theological point* may not be imposed upon the *historical meaning* of Genesis 2:2.Certainly Hebrews applies Genesis 2:2 to the argument for an ongoing and/or eschatological sabbath; but he does so only *typologically*. His argument in Hebrews 4:4 no more proves the *original* day in Genesis 2:2 is ongoing, than his typological proof for Christ's eternity in Hebrews 7 proves Melchizedek actually lacked human genealogy. There he argues that Christ has an ongoing existence by alluding to Genesis' not providing a genealogy for Melchizedek (Heb 7:3). This does not prove that the original revelation regarding historical Melchizedek actually indicates he had no earthly lineage. This is typological argument; it is not *expositing* the text's original meaning, but *extending* it. This is all the more significant in that even some Framework advocates admit Hebrews 4 is a "notoriously difficult passage" (Blocher, 56). We must agree with Young: "There is no Scriptural warrant whatever (certainly not Hebrews 4:3-5) for the idea that this seventh day is eternal" (Young, 77 n73).

The attempt to suggest John 5:17 into the debate only shows the deficiency of non-traditional, literary views of Genesis. For instance, Irons writes: "John 5:17 also implies that God's Sabbath is eternal. . . . If the Father is working on the Sabbath 'until now,' then his Sabbath also must continue 'until now'" (Irons, 51 n113; cf. Kline, "Space and Time," 10; Blocher, 57). Two immediate problems arise upon this exposition of John 5:17: (a) the problem of internal contradiction; and (b) the problem of eternal creation.

a.) The problem of internal contradiction. The question naturally arises then: *Did God cease from labor on the sabbath, or not?* On the literal construction resulting from the traditional and confessional exegesis, Genesis 2:2-3 informs us that he did in fact cease from labor *on that particular day*. Only on the literal analysis, then, can we avoid the contradiction inherent in the eternal Genesis 2 sabbath position, for in the eternal sabbath view God *does* cease from labor on his sabbath and God does *not* cease from labor. Actually though, Jesus is here referring to the weekly recurring earthly sabbath, noting that God himself works on it (e.g., through Jesus in healing and so forth).

b.) The problem of eternal creation. Is the Framework Hypothesis willing to argue consistently from their approach to John 5:17? That is, on Jesus' statement here, they argue God's original Sabbath mentioned in Genesis 2 continues. Therefore, by parity of reasoning Jesus' statement that "the Father is *working*" would seem to demand that he is *still* creating the universe.

(2) The eternal sabbath argument can be turned in upon itself. As Harris himself puts it: "The seventh day is presented as very special. Unlike the others, it has no conclusion mentioned. There was no evening to it and no morning leading to anything else. God rested from his creative activity"(Harris, 109). Kline agrees: "In the Genesis prologue the unending nature of God's Sabbath is signalized by the absence of the evening-morning formula from the account of the seventh day" (Kline, "Space and Time," 10). The Majority Report concurs: "The day that ends the creation week is clearly not a literal 24-hour day, even though it also is referred to by the name 'day.' It has neither evening nor morning. It is eternal" (Majority Report, 7). Consequently, if we accept the implications of such an argument, then the seventh day *differs* from the preceding six in a way that *demands* the preceding days *were in fact* literal! For the first six days *are* most definitely limited by the "evening/morning" refrain.

(3) Grammatical reasons, though, suggest the necessity for the lack of the "evening/morning" refrain on Day Sev5en. As Cassuto notes: "whenever clear reference is made to the relationship between a given day and the next, it is precisely sunrise that is accounted the beginning of the second day" (Cassuto, 28).[40] Since the week of God's creating is ended, that is, since God's original creative activity has "ceased" (this matter is emphasized by three-fold repetition in Ge 2:2-3), no following creational day in the series is expected or prepared for. Hence, the dropping of the "evening/morning" marker on the seventh day: that series of days has ended forever. The sabbath is the *seventh* in the *sequence* of creation days, even though no like days follow, in that creation is a unique period in earth history.[41]

---

[40] See also: Ernest Kevan, "Genesis," in *New Bible Commentary*, ed., Francis Davidson (Grand Rapids: Eerdmans, 1954), 77.

[41] Pipa suggests that the day may also be left open-ended intentionally, allowing it to serve (much like Melchizedek's lack of genealogy) as a *type* of the eternal sabbath. Pipa, 169.

(4) Kline asserts that "in the beginning" is a non-temporal, upper register matter and the sabbath is also a timeless, upper level reality. Therefore the six days of creation are upper level (divine, timeless) realities, since "the six days are part of the same strand as the seventh day, and the 'beginning'" (Kline, "Space and Time," 10). In that he is mistaken on the sabbath question, his argument falls to the ground. But even if he were correct, the days in between would then be distinguished from the sabbath day by the various calendrical limitations not associated with Day Seven. Besides, does not the *beginning*, which he mentions, initiate temporal reality where time *is relevant*? Is not the sun on Day 4 designated as a temporal ruler to mark off the passing of time?

(5) This view of an eternal sabbath based on the sabbath day of Genesis 2:2 contradicts Exodus 20:9-11. There God commands us to observe a weekly sabbath after six days of work for the express purpose of *imitating* him in his original creative week. As the Westminster Standards put it: "The seventh day is the sabbath of the Lord thy God: from the *example of God*, who in six days made heaven and earth, the sea, and all that in them is, and rested the seventh day" (LC 120b; cp. also SC 62). The *original* sabbath *day* (Ge 2:3) was a literal day following upon six prior literal days. Again, since the "sabbath day" is the seventh in a series of six preceding literal days, how can we interpret it other than literally?

(6) Furthermore, God does not bless *his eternal rest*, but *a particular day* in the temporal realm where his creative work is finally concluded, being ended with the divine appreciation, "behold, it was very good" (1:31). If the "sabbath day" *of Genesis 2:2-3* is ongoing, it would imply no fall and curse, for then God would be continually hallowing and blessing that "ongoing day," that is, all of time from that moment to this.

The Long Day Problem (Gen. 2:4)

Objection: Genesis 2:4 reads: "This is the account of the heavens and the earth when they were created, in the day that the Lord God made earth and heaven" (NASB). Evidently, as some argue, this speaks of the entire creation week as a "day," showing that "day" may not be a term applying to a literal 24-hour time frame. For instance, Hyers writes: "The six-day account of Genesis 1—2:4a and the single day account of Genesis 2:4b and following hardly agree in time-frame, sequence, or detail."[42]   This is especially significant in that it is found in the creation account itself.

Response: (1) In this verse the word *yom* appears in a prepositional phrase: *bᵉyom* (בְּיוֹם). This phrase involves a preposition in construct with an infinitive forming a temporal conjunction. This adverbial construction is an idiomatic expression meaning "when." This is widely recognized among Hebrew grammarians. For instance: "The construction *bᵉyom* + inf. 'on the day when' = 'at the time when' = 'as/when'. . . (e.g., Gen 2:4 'at the time when the Lord God made the earth and heaven')."[43] Even Day Age advocates admit this idiomatic expression does not militate against the literal day view.[44]   Several notable translations treat it thus: NIV, NRSV, NAB. For instance, the NIV reads: "This is the account of the heavens and the earth when they were created. *When* the Lord God made the earth and the heavens."

(2) Even if Genesis 2:4 did use "day" in a different sense, this would not undermine the meaning of the first chapter. Genesis 1 carefully qualifies its creative days in various ways (see points 2-4 above); such qualifications are lacking in Genesis 2:4.

---

[42] Hyers, *The Meaning of Creation*, 40.

[43] Jenni and Westermann, *Theological Lexicon of the Old Testament*, 2:529. They note that this usage "occurs over 60x." See also: Francis Brown, S. R. Driver, C. A. *Briggs, Hebrew and English Lexicon of the Old Testament* (Oxford: Clarendon, 1972), 400. *Theological Wordbook of the Old Testament*, 1:851. *Theological Dictionary of the Old Testament*, 6:15.Cassuto, *Genesis,* 1:99, 100.

[44] "I would rather argue that *bᵉyom* of Gen. 2:4 is a prepositional phrase simply meaning an indefinite 'when.'" Harris, 109.

Chapter 3

A REBUTTAL OF THE FRAMEWORK HYPOTHESIS
Kenneth L. Gentry, Jr.

Introduction

Numerous arguments have been offered in attempting to substantiate the Framework Hypothesis. Many of these are basically disputes *against* the traditional, historical, confessional view of Genesis 1, rather than arguments *for* the Hypothesis itself. Space constraints forbid a response to each and every argument. They even preclude a *thorough* analysis of the basic arguments. Nevertheless, an *adequate* response can be presented in summary fashion against the foundational principles of the Hypothesis.

Foundational Issues

Once again, I appreciate the yeoman work of Irons in conveniently organizing, summarizing, presenting, and defending what surely are the three key arguments for the Framework Hypothesis (Irons, 27-52).[1] Consequently, Irons' presentation will provide the structure for my critique.

Irons declares that "there are three exegetical arguments for the framework interpretation." Summarily stated and employing abbreviated descriptions of Irons' presentation, these are: (1) The triad argument. "The intentional literary design of the text, as reflected in the symmetry of the two triads" (Irons, 27). (2) The providential argument. That which "Gen. 2:5-6 establishes regarding the mode of divine providence during the creation week" shows that the "creative acts are not narrated sequentially" (Irons, 27). (3) The cosmogony argument. "The specifically metaphorical nature of these non-literal days is given a coherent explanation within the broader context of the Bible's two-register cosmological teaching" (Irons, 27).

Certainly these three arguments serve as a set of "keys to the kingdom," as it were, granting access to any who would enter into the framework world of "kingdoms and kings" in Genesis 1.

---

[1] Section titled: "Three Exegetical Arguments."

Irons forthrightly declares that the triad structure is "the primary exegetical basis of the framework interpretation" (Irons, 27). Kline suggests that "the literary character" involving "parallelism" serves to "compel the conclusion" of a "figurative chronological framework for the account" (Kline, "Rain," 156). Indeed, this feature provides "confirmation" of the framework approach (Kline, "Rain," 157).

And certainly Framework advocates deem crucial the evidence drawn from Genesis 2:5-6. When Kline first developed and presented his new exegetical insight, he noted that he had formulated the "decisive word against the traditional interpretation" (Kline, "Rain," 148). He insists it is the "conclusive exegetical evidence . . . that prevents anyone who follows the analogy of Scripture from supposing that Genesis 1 teaches a creation in the space of six solar days."[2] Futato speaks of features of his exegesis of Genesis 2 as "foundational," playing a "major role," and serving as a "key to understanding" the framework approach to creation. Irons proclaims it as an "exegetical conviction" for the view (Irons, 27).

Regarding the less familiar and more complex, esoteric foundation stone, Kline insists of his two-register cosmogony argument that "this idea developed into the main point and has become the umbrella under which the other, restated arguments are accorded an ancillary place here and there" (Kline, "Space and Time,"1). Irons deems Kline's two-register paper to be "the most comprehensive and convincing exegetical defense of the framework interpretation available" (Irons, 36).

Before we actually engage the arguments, we should note some surprising matters regarding these "three exegetical arguments" as we consider foundational concerns.

Foundational Concerns

Despite these summary elements of the Framework Hypothesis being vigorously presented, complications arise in establishing the innovative theological system on these foundation stones.

---

[2] Meredith G. Kline, "Review of *The Christian View of Science and Scripture*," *Westminster Theological Journal* 18:1 (November, 1955): 54.

Foundational erosion. As noted above, Framework advocates frequently point to these foundation stones as securing their theological house. Nevertheless, these stones appear to be made of shifting sand rather than solid rock. Indeed, not one stone here shall be left upon another, which will not be torn down.

Although the *triad framework* gives the hermeneutical system "its name," *immediately* upon mentioning this as the "first" point in the "positive exegetical basis," Irons admits: "By itself, this does not prove beyond a reasonable doubt that the days are non-literal, or that the narrative is topical." Rather, we discover, it leaves "that impression" (Irons, 27). In fact, this results from a problem he admits later: "Certainly it is possible to acknowledge the presence of a schematic element in Gen. 1 and yet to argue that a non-literal, non-sequential interpretation is an additional logical step that does not necessarily follow" (Irons, 29). Kline confesses that the matter of proper chronology in Genesis 1 must "be an open exegetical question," which, in his opinion, is "actually closed by the exegetical evidence of Gen. 2:5" (Kline, "Rain," 157).

Framework disciples point to the most ornate stone of the house that Kline built — the *two-register cosmogony* stone — and proclaim, as it were, "behold what a wonderful stone and what a wonderful building." But when we turn to consider this stone, we are surprised to learn from Irons that "one may or may not be persuaded of this particular aspect of Kline's argument and still be able to hold the framework interpretation itself" (Irons, 3). In fact, this feature of the system is seldom mentioned outside of a tight circle of Kline disciples (e.g., Thompson, Ross, and Blocher do not employ it). Interestingly, this "umbrella" argument (Kline, "Space and Time," 1) was (wisely, we believe) not mentioned in the presbytery's Majority Report.

Consequently, after stripping away the non-essentials, we are really left with their exegesis of Genesis 2:5. But this presents us with a new frustration regarding the novelty of the argument.

Foundational novelty. Admittedly a deep suspicion runs among traditional exegetes that the Framework Hypothesis arose among evangelicals as a new option in the creation debate only *after* the challenge of evolution presented itself. (Framework advocates would dismiss this as a *post hoc phenomenon.*) Not only so, but the Framework Hypothesis presents us with a moving target, with various new features arising from time to time.

The originator of the Framework view among reformed evangelicals was Arie Noordtzij (1924). Thirty years after Noordtzij's work, and despite the deep, broad, and long-standing interest in and debate over Genesis 1-3, Meredith Kline published an innovative exegetical analysis of Genesis 2:5 (1958[3]), which Blocher calls "a new argument" from one "who is not afraid to leave the beaten track" (Blocher, 53). More recently, Mark Futato published a further development on Kline's research on Genesis 2:5. Futato promotes his "new insights" on the text "which have not yet been set forth" (Futato, 1, 2). Thus, the last Framework Hypothesis foundation stone remaining after discarding the non-essential ones, is a novelty. Now forty years later Kline weaves for us a new theological construct, the two-register cosmogony (1996). Kline presents his latest research as "adding something somewhat fresh to the old debate" (Kline, "Space and Time," 1). A foundational portion of this new theological argument is his innovative view of the theophanic presence of God in Genesis 1:2-3 which allows him to "start fresh" ("Glory," 250) and that encourages his discovery of "a key new element" ("Glory," 250) in the creation record.

Foundational difficulty. What is more, the absolutely essential providential argument is derived from Genesis 2:5-6. This passage, according to Kidner, contains several "words of debatable meaning" and inheres with a "difficulty" that is "reflected in the variety of interpretations that have been put forward" (Kidner, "Wet or Dry?,"109, 11). The Framework Hypothesis, then, is dependent upon a new and innovative exposition of a passage noted for its difficulty and which contains ambiguous terms. And despite Kline's approach being around for forty years, when we search into the standard commentaries we look in vain for his providence-and-aridity argument. As I will show below a more plausible and widely held view is readily available, making the unique Framework conclusions wholly unnecessary, while preserving the "majestic march of days" in Genesis 1 and shamelessly affirming "unnecessary supernaturalism" on at least one occasion during the creation week.

---

[3] Kline already had this in mind as early as 1955, though leaving it unpublished until the 1958 *Westminster Theological Journal* article. See: Kline, Review of Bernard Ramm, 54.

Presentation of Critique

Having established the basics of the Framework argument, I will now analyze and critique it. The surface appearance of the triad is appealing, and initially somewhat persuasive. But it ultimately fails of its purpose, as I will show.

Triad Symmetry as Topic Organizer

Triad Symmetry Introduction. We must remember that it is "primarily" because of this triadic structure "that the term 'framework' has been attached to the position" (Irons, 28). It is argued that the triadic parallelism between the first three days and the last three indicates a *topical* rather than chronological arrangement, as represented in the following table published in the Majority Report (p. 6).

DOMAINS	RULERS
Day 1 Light	Day 4 Luminaries

Day 2   Sky
          Seas
	Day 5 Sea creatures
	          Winged creatures

Day 3 Dry land Day 3b Vegetation	Day 6 Land animals Day 6b Man
THE RULER OF ALL Day 7 Sabbath	

This is all very nice and neat.[4] And it certainly is quite an interesting alignment. But as noted above this does not prove the non-chronological nature of Genesis 1, for "not all" who recognize the symmetric arrangement of the divine creative activity "espouse the framework interpretation" (Irons, 29; see for example: Cassuto, 42; Young, 69; Kelly, 201). In fact, not only do some chronological sequence adherents affirm the symmetry, but Framework advocates admit that "a non-literal, non-sequential

---

[4] We must note the chiastic relationship between the events of Day 2 and Day 5 does not contradict the arrangement.

71

interpretation is an additional logical step that does not necessarily follow" (Irons, 29).

But other triad problems weaken the Framework Hypothesis. The Framework system reminds us of the duck that appears to be gliding effortlessly across the pond. But underneath the water's surface, a whole lot of fancy footwork is going on.

Triad Symmetry Confusion. Even among advocates of a literary, framework approach to Genesis 1, we find confusion over the model. This sort of problem should not surprise us, for literary framework advocate Wenham notes: "The arrangement of 1:1 — 2:3 is itself highly problematic. Briefly, the eight works of creation are prompted by ten divine commands and executed on six different days. Many attempts have been made to discover a simpler, more symmetrical arrangement underlying the present scheme. None of these suggestions has proved persuasive" (Wenham, 6). This leads S. E. McEvenue to speak of the "dissymetric symmetry" of Genesis 1.[5]

Reformed Framework theologian Willem Van Gemeren speaks of the "dissonance" within the creation account where "on the one hand, the fourth day belongs to the formative aspect of God's creation (days 1-3) and, on the other hand, it is part of the filling of the created world (days 4-6)" (Van Gemeren, 45). Thus, from one perspective Day 4 is attached to the formative part of creation along with Days 1-3, thereby seeing Days 1-4 as related. From another angle Day 4 is attached to the latter days of creation, forming a set of Days 4-6.

Illustrating the disagreement among Framework advocates, Van Gemeren accurately presents a slightly different scheme. But in his being *more* accurate, he fails to be *totally* accurate, and both precision problems expose a flaw in the alleged artistic symmetry. Notice that he (correctly) has the "seas" created on Day 3 (cp. Ge 1:10), which contradicts the Majority Report's schema (Majority Report, 6). It also throws off the balance with Day 5 (which doesn't take all the evidence into account on the part of the Majority Report) because the aquatic creatures are then placed in "the seas" (1:22). Notice also that the water which will eventually form the seas is not

---

[5] S. E. McEvenue, *The Narrative Style of the Priestly Writer* (Rome: Pontifical Institute, 1971), 113-15. Cited in Wenham, 6.

created on Day 2, it already exists on Day 1 (Ge 1:2); even Kline admits that Genesis 1:2 is a part of Day 1.[6] VanGemeren's diagram is presented thus:[7]

Formation of the World	Filling of the World
Day 1 darkness, light	Day 4 heavenly light-bearers
Day 2 heavens, water	Day 5 birds of the air; water animals
Day 3 seas, land, vegetation	Day 6 land animals; man; provision of food

Wenham's analysis even suggests the waters are insignificant, for he neither portrays them in his table nor mentions them in his explanation:

Day 1 Light	Day 4 Luminaries
Day 2 Sky	Day 5 Birds and Fish
Day 3 Land (Plants)	Day 6 Animals and Man (Plants for food)
Day 7 Sabbath	

The triad structure appears to be malleable according to need: it attempts to be all things to all people. Embarrassing features may be overlooked (Wenham), re-arranged (Majority Report), or presented warts and all (VanGemeren). As presented to our presbytery, the Framework position absolutely misconstrues what Moses actually says. Here the tabular error is openly declared as fact in the text: "God creates the sky and seas on Day 2" (p. 6). That is wholly mistaken; and serves as evidence of the error of the triadic structure. We expressly read of the *third day* that God separated the land and the water, gathering the water "into one place" and *only then* naming this body of water "the seas" (Ge 1:10). Remember: two

---

[6] Kline's heading shows that Day 1 is contained in Ge 1:1-5; and the text specifically declares it, when he comments that we must understand "*the beginning* as the commencement of the seven-day history." Kline, "Genesis," 82. See also: Young, 87, 104.

[7] It also is the scheme presented in Mathews, 115-116.

pages previous in the Majority Report, our Framework brothers emphasize the significance of "naming" (p. 4) — apparently unless it undercuts their position.

Triad Symmetry Imbalance. The Framework Hypothesis works on the assumption of a topical arrangement rather than a chronological arrangement of the material of Genesis 1. It suggests that "obvious" balance and parallel between Days 1-3 and Days 4-6 is clear evidence of the overriding *topical* nature of Moses' concern. Unfortunately, the proposed hypothetical, non-chronological framework for Genesis 1 fails structurally and logically, as has been noted since the days of Keil and Delitzsch: "The work of creation does not fall, as *Herder* and others maintain, into two triads of days, with the work of the second answering to that of the first."[8] It possesses only an apparent and superficial parallelism, a parallelism that can be equally accounted for, if need be, by the providential action of God in creation.

What is worse, this interpretive procedure overthrows the obvious chronological development revealed in Genesis 1. This is a serious methodological flaw in the Framework hermeneutic in that Genesis 1 provides both the revelational explanation of the universe and the world, as well as to the historical revelation of the development of the human race and of redemption in Genesis, which in turn is foundational to the theology and redemptive history of all of Scripture.

The "dissonance" in Genesis 1 leads to problems of severe imbalance in the proposed triad — which may help explain why Framework advocates admit the parallelism does not prove their point (see previous point). The dissonance is deafening. Numerous discordant features mar the supposed literary framework.

The arrangement not only fails symmetrically, but it also neglects to account for and organize all features of the six day revelation. For instance, as Kline, Young, and others note, "the waters" are created on Day 1 (Ge 1:2), not Day 2.[9] Consequently, Day 4 lacks an appropriate parallel inhabitant for the waters.

---

[8] Keil and Delitzsch, 38.

[9] Ge 1:1 stands "as the commencement of the seven-day history," Kline, "Genesis," 82. Young, 104. Kelly, 79.

In addition, Genesis informs us that the creatures produced on Day 5 are to swim in the "seas" (יַמִּים , *yammim*) which were formed *not* on the parallel Day 2 but established (even *named!*) on Day 3. These creatures are to "fill the waters of the *seas*" (1:22) and are called "fish of the *seas*" (1:26, 28). In addition to the problem mentioned in the preceding paragraph, this results in the "seas" separated out on Day 3 having no corresponding inhabitant created on its "parallel" day, Day 6. No wonder Ridderbos urges that the problem of the fish in the seas "must not be given much weight" (Ridderbos, 34-35). The whole schema is exposed as erroneous by such discoveries.

Furthermore, the birds created on Day 5 require the prior upthrusting of the continental land masses on Day 3, thereby failing to parallel Day 2: the birds are commanded to "multiply on the *earth*" (1:22). Besides, this also leaves the creation of the "waters above the expanse" on Day 2 without an inhabitant on its parallel Day 5. The original waters of Day 1 and the waters above the expanse are being lost in the shuffle.

Still further, the birds are called the "birds of the *sky*" (Ge 1:26, 28). That is, their unique sphere of operation is the "expanse" or "firmament," which was *named* "heaven" or "sky" (שָׁמַיִם , *shamayim*) on Day 2. Thus, the creation of the birds assumes in the literary process the prior existence of the "heaven" of Day 2 as well as the "earth" of Day 3. That is, they assume the sequential progress of Genesis 1.

We must wonder why Framework advocates deem the "problem" of the sun's creation on a literal, chronological Day 4 to be a stumbling block for the reader? Why should this be a concern, since the fish and birds are left without their proper habitats in terms of the literary arrangement of the material? Of course, none of these problems affect the common-sense, historically-promoted, traditionally-held, chronological approach.

Other dissonant features of the alleged artistry of Genesis 1 include Days 3 and 6 being emphasized by each possessing two acts of creation (as opposed to one act on each of the other days), two announcements of "And God said" (Ge 1:9, 11, 24, 26), and two benedictions (Ge 1:10, 12, 25, 31). Yet Days 4 and 6 are emphasized by their wordiness — these two days receiving far more discussion by Moses than the other days. And we must remember that according to Van Gemeren, Day 4 is a member of the first set of days (Days 1-4) *and* the second set (Days 4-6). And Day 4 also allegedly "recapitulates" Day 1. This all becomes very confusing.

An interesting feature that has frustrated modern commentators (as well as the Jewish translators of the Septuagint) is the disharmony of numerical features: "the eight works of creation are prompted by ten divine commands and executed on six different days" (Wenham, 6). Also, we find God uttering blessings on Days 5-7, but not on Days 1-4. We note that the fulfillment formula of the first day differs from that of the other five days: "And there was *x*" (once) versus "and it was so" (six times). The formula of execution usually precedes the formula of appreciation, but in verse 4 it follows it. The fourth day differs from the other creative days in that it "is the only day on which no divine word subsequent to the fulfillment is added" (Wenham, 23). Rather than representing the picturesque smile of Mona Lisa, they cause the confused frowns of Many Literalists. (See "Table of Discordant Features on the next page.)

Table of Discordant Features in the Framework

Kingdoms / Realm		Kings / Rulers	
D a y 1	1) Absolute creation (Gn 1:1-2; cp. Ex 20:11) 2) Waters exist (Gn 1:2) 3) Light 4) Light 5) Light *fills* space 6) Creation by fiat alone	**D a y 4**	1) No corresponding element 2) No corresponding inhabitant-king 3) Lightbearers (but placed *in "firmament"* [3x] created on D2 [5x]) 4) Lightbearers assigned "rule" (Gn 1:16, 18; differs from D5) 5) Lightbearers *exist* (fill/exist order differs D2/5; D3/6) 6) Creation by fiat *and* making. 7) Wordy emphasis of D4 (not D3 to correspond with lengthy D6) 8) Strong palistrophic chiasm pattern (lacking on D1)
D a y 2	1) Firmament 2) Waters of D1 separated to above firmament 3) Waters of D1 separated to below firmament 4) Waters 5) Waters *exist* 6) Firmament 7) Firmament *exists*	**D a y 5**	1) Birds fly in firmament (but "multiply" "on the earth," Gn 1:22) 2) No corresponding inhabitant-king 3) Water creatures (but in "seas" [1:22, 26, 28] of D3) ("waters" already exist on D1 [1:2]) 4) Water creatures *not* assigned rule 5) Water creatures *"fill"* the seas 6) Birds not assigned "rule" 7) Birds *fill* ("multiply") — but "on the earth" (1:22)
D a y 3	1) Seas 2) Dry land 3) Vegetation 4) Seas *exist* 5) Dry land *exists* 6) No wordy emphasis corresponding to D6 (D4 instead)	**D a y 6**	1) No corresponding inhabitant-king 2) Beasts and man inhabit; but only man rules. 3) No corresponding element 4) Sea creatures *fill* ("teem") the seas 5) Man *"fills"* the earth 6) Wordy emphasis of D6 (like on D4)

Furthermore we should note the inconsistent linguistic symmetry in the creation account, as well. Due to space pressures I will suggest these in tabular format. Some of these have been presented before, but this format allows a quick glance to reveal disruptions of patterns that undercut any literary artistry in the order of the Framework Hypothesis.

Inconsistent Linguistic Symmetry in Genesis 1 — 2:3

	Day 1	Day 2	Day 3	Day 4	Day 5	Day 6	Day 7
"And God said"	1	1	2	1	1	4	—
"Let there be"	1	2	3	1	2	2	—
"And it was so"	—	1	2	1	—	2	—
Description of divine act	—	1	1	2	1	2	—
Divine naming	1	1	2	—	—	---	—
Divine blessing	—	—	—	—	1	1	1
Declaration "good"	1	—	2	1	1	1	—
"Evening & morning"	1	1	1	1	1	1	—

Triad Symmetry Chronology. The supposed symmetry in Genesis 1 does not overthrow the historic exegesis. Traditional interpreters frequently recognize the parallel (!) between divine design and historical fact. As Young observed long ago: "The fact that some of the material in Genesis one is given in schematic form, it does not necessarily follow that what is stated is to be dismissed as figurative or as not describing what actually occurred. . . . Nor does it even suggest, that the days are to be taken in a non-chronological sense" (Young, 65-66). As reformed theologian Jean-Marc Berthoud reminds Henri Blocher: "What difficulty would it be for [the Author of the Universe] to cause the most complex, refined literary form to coincide with the very way in which He Himself created all things in six days. Artistic form is in no sense opposed to an actual relation of facts, especially since the Author of the account is none less than the actual Creator of the facts which are described in that account."[10]

The God of creation is a God of beauty, order, and design. He can create in a literal chronological manner which also utilizes symmetric design. For instance, just as the dry land arose from beneath the primal waters and bore life (vegetation) on the third day, so Christ the Lord arose from the tomb to newness of life on the third day. Both are historically true, though an interesting parallel exists between them. As James Jordan notes, in John 20:15 Mary Magdalene sees Jesus, the Second Adam, in a garden (John 19:41) and supposes that he is the gardener. This suggests to the student of Scripture a new Eve, restored from her sins, encountering the New Adam in the new garden of the new covenant. This theological imagery paralleling the original creation structure may very well be true here. But she really did see the resurrected Jesus in a literal garden.[11]

We must not allow the *stylistic harmony* in the *revelation* of creation to override the *emphatic progress* in the *history* of creation. The chronological succession leaves too deep an impression upon the narrative to be mere ornamentation. Besides, as I note above most of the events of creation week demand the particular chronological order presented. This logical progress establishes a pattern of temporal development. Those one or two features that do not seem to be required in their particular order, nevertheless appear within the flow of carefully structured chronological progress and do not logically contradict it. The revealed pattern shows a clear preparation of earth for man. Man's habitat is set in place, then man appears.

Framework advocates frequently argue — as does the Majority Report (p. 44) — that "dischronology" is a frequent element employed by biblical writers (e.g., Irons, 13-15). They even cite examples from Genesis 2, in the very context of our debate. What seems to escape them due to their strong commitment to their Hypothesis is: Dischronology does *not* occur in texts that expressly affirm historical sequence — as evidenced in the very samples they present. Genesis 1 is so carefully sequenced that Kidner reminds us: "the march of the days is too majestic a progress to carry no

---

[10] Cited in Kelly, 115. See also: Weeks, 107.

[11] James B. Jordan, *Creation in Six Days: A Defense of the Traditional Reading of Genesis One* (Moscow, Ida.: Canon Press, 1999).

implication of ordered sequence" (Kidner, 54-55). Admitting dischronology as a literary device in general, does not prove it is the literary point of Genesis 1 in particular. Such an argument commits the informal logical fallacy of sweeping generalization.

One illustration of Kline's literary approach to Genesis, for instance, dovetails perfectly with the sequential view of the traditional interpretation. Kline writes: "another literary interest at work within this parallelism is that of achieving climax, as is done, for example, in introducing men after all other creatures as their king" (Kline, "Rain," 114). This "literary interest" happens also to present Adam as *God's* climax in his literal creation, not just *Moses'* climax in his literary production.

The fundamental problem for the traditional exegesis, according to the Framework Hypothesis, is the relationship of Days 1 and 4. As Futato argues: "Days 1 and 4 are two different perspective on the same creative work" (Futato, 16). Irons agrees: "Days 1 and 4 do not describe separate activities of God, separated by three days, but contemporaneous activities described from different perspectives" (Majority Report, 6; cf., Irons, 58). This creates a problem by compounding two fiats into one: the creation of light and the creation of the luminaries; or else it makes two fiats result in only one effect. (For more detail on this problem, see later Chapter by Butler.)

Triad Symmetry Error. In many of the writings of Framework proponents, the triad of days is sorted out into two classes, either Realm and Ruler, Kingdoms and Kings, or, as the Majority Report presents it (less aesthetically!): Domains and Rulers (p. 6). Irons, following his mentor Kline, prefers "Creation Kingdoms" and "Creature Kings" in that "the concepts of dominion and kingship are prominent in Gen. 1:1-2:3. In each of the days of the second triad, the created entities are assigned a ruling task" (Irons, 28. Cf. Kline, "Genesis," 82; Kline, "Space and Time," 5, 9).

This alleged structure of Genesis 1 promotes a false view of both the creation results and the creation record. This creates a problem for two reasons, one linguistic and one theological.

Linguistically, we must observe that the animals are not appointed "rule." Nowhere does the text mention that they are to rule. Their command to "be fruitful and multiply" in the earth is not tantamount to a command to rule. After all, the plants of Day 3 are designed also to "bear fruit" and "seed" and thereby multiply, *but they do not rule.* Irons writes: "The fish and birds of day five are blessed with a dominion mandate that implies rule over the spheres established by day two: 'Be fruitful and multiply, and fill the waters in the seas, and let birds multiply on the earth' (1:23). This 'be fruitful and multiply" mandate closely parallels the mandate given to man (1:26, 28) and is therefore to be understood in similar terms, as a dominion mandate" (Irons, 28-29). This fallacious reasoning succumbs to a *reductio ad absurdum*: by parity of reasoning we could likewise infer that the luminaries are to be fruitful and multiply because they are, like man, given a dominion mandate!

The Framework assertion here is another extension of the serious methodological problem we have with the Hypothesis: it constantly reads things into the text which are not there (see the incredible description of God "going to work" in the Majority Report, p. 8 [cited above], and my further response below). The notion of animal rule is simply alien to the text; it must be imposed upon the text.

Theologically, only *man* is to rule. In fact, he is to rule *over the sea, air, and land creatures* (Ge 1:26, 28). God *expressly* declares this. And could easily have employed similar language had he intended a ruling function for the animals; but he does not. The psalmist is absorbed in praise when he recognizes *man's* rule over the animal kingdom (Ps 8). Nowhere is man to share rule with the animals; man names the animals as he begins exercising his rule over them (Ge 2:20). In fact, an important feature in the historical fall of Adam is Adam's allowing the animal realm (the serpent) to exercise rule over him! Rather than Genesis 1 suggesting Realm-Ruler relations, the text actually reinforces man's uniqueness on the earth in this regard. In fact, this appears to be the very point of Genesis 1 — as well as Psalm 8.

Triad Symmetry Argument. Even if there is as much literary structure as Framework advocates contend, what does that prove? Blocher suggests that it at least proves that Genesis 1 should not be taken chronologically: "But could this extremely careful construction of the narrative not coincide with the chronological reality of the divine work, as certain literalists attempt to plead? Of course, you can always imagine anything. But, in the face of what the author shows of his method, there is no reason to suppose it" (Blocher, 53).

His reason for this is somewhat obscure: "The hypothesis of the literary procedure gives sufficient explanation of the form of the text; anything further would be superfluous. Occam's razor, the principle of economy which argued against the multiplication of hypotheses, removes ideas of this kind. The suggestion betrays the a priori desire to find literal language" (Blocher, 53). His argument seems to be that because the dischronology hypothesis is the simplest hypothesis in explaining the literary structure, there is no reason to think the text is chronological. But there are several problems with such reasoning.

First, he does not correctly apply Occam's Razor. Occam's Razor suggests that when two explanations are equally good (they both explicate the explanandum), the simpler one is to be preferred. For example, if your car will not start, two explanations may account for the problem. Explanation 1 proposes a dead battery; Explanation 2, both a dead battery and gremlins. Occam's Razor would choose the simpler explanation, Explanation 1.

Now back to our problem. It is difficult to determine which of the two views in question is the simplest explanation of Genesis 1 having a certain literary structure. The Framework Hypothesis argues the explanation that this text has literary structure, which indicates dischronology. The traditional interpreters counter by arguing the explanation that this text has a literary structure which emphasizes how God prepared the world for man to inhabit. But which is the simplest explanation? The issue does not lend itself to this type of analysis.

Even if the Framework Hypothesis could be shown to be the simpler view, it would only be preferred if all things were equal. In other words, if there were no other considerations involved. But as noted above, this is clearly not the case. Framework opponent Weeks' comments are insightful: "A theologically structured history presupposes a God who actively shapes history so that it conforms to his plan. A liberal exegete who denies the existence of such a God must dismiss as true history all biblical accounts which see theological patterns in history. The evangelical has no basis for such an a priori dismissal of structured history. The fact that Genesis 1 displays a structure in no way prejudices its claim to historicity."[12] Once again, Kidner insists that "the march of the days is too majestic a progress to carry no implication of ordered sequence" (Kidner, 54).

---

[12] Noel Weeks, "The Hermeneutical Problem of Genesis 1-11." *Themelios* 4.1 (Sept. 1978): 18.

Furthermore, appeals to economy of explanation prove too much. One could argue (as some do) that the best explanation for the literary structure is that the whole of Genesis 1 is to be taken figuratively — the chronology, as well as the events described. This obviously is a bridge too far.

In addition, to argue that literary structure (e.g. parallelism) implies dischronology is fallacious. For example, Exodus 7-13:17 contains parallelism and yet reports chronological progress. It contains three cycles of plagues with three plagues each and then a tenth plague. As James B. Jordan reminds us: "The first plague of each cycle begins with a command to go to Pharaoh in the morning. The second in each cycle begins with a simple command to go to Pharaoh. The third in each cycle is not announced to Pharaoh at all."[13]

Young is surely correct when he observes:

> In the first place, from the fact that some of the material in Genesis one is given in schematic form, it does not necessarily follow that what is stated is to be dismissed as figurative or as not describing what actually occurred. Sometimes a schematic arrangement may serve the purpose of emphasis. Whether the language is figurative or symbolical, however, must be determined upon exegetical grounds. Secondly, a schematic disposition of the material in Genesis one does not prove, not does it even suggest, that the days are to be taken in a non-chronological sense. There appears to be a certain schematization, for example, in the genealogies of Matthew one, but it does not follow that the names of the genealogies are to be understood in a non-chronological sense, or that Matthew teaches that the generations from Abraham to David parallel, or were contemporary with, those from David to the Babylonian captivity and that these in turn are paralleled to the generations from the Babylonian captivity to Christ.... Why, then, must we conclude that, merely because of a schematic arrangement, Moses has disposed of Chronology? (Young, 65-66)

As noted previously, even Kline admits that the literary structure of Genesis 1 does not prove dischronology: "Whether the events narrated occurred in the order of their narration would, as far as the chronological framework of Genesis 1 is concerned, be an open exegetical question" (Kline, "Rain, 157).

---

[13] Jordan, *Creation in Six Days.*

Conclusion. The triad argument for the Framework Hypothesis has been weighed in the balance and found wanting. This is especially significant in that a strong, textually-derived, historically-affirmed, Confession-secured case exists for God's acting "in the beginning, to create, or make of nothing, the world, and all things therein whether visible or invisible, *in the space of six days*; and all very good" (WCF 4:1). We believe the traditional, literal, reformed interpretation of Genesis 1 is superior to the literary interpretation of the Framework Hypothesis.

Ordinary Providence as Creational Mechanism

Introduction. I come now to what Kline deems the "decisive word against the traditional interpretation" (Kline, "Rain," 148). The Framework exposition of Genesis 2:5. That famous text reads: "Now no shrub of the field was yet in the earth, and no plant of the field had yet sprouted, for the Lord God had not sent rain upon the earth; and there was no man to cultivate the ground."

But what does this lone verse teach that leads the Majority Report so confidently to declare "introduces a principle" that "must affect how we understand everything that has gone before" (Majority Report, 9)?

Excerpts from Kline will inform us of the utility of this verse for the Framework Hypothesis:

> Embedded in Gen. 2:5 ff. is the principle that the *modus operandi* of the divine providence was the same during the creation period as that of ordinary providence at the present time. . . . In contradiction to Gen. 2:5, the twenty-four-hour day theory must presuppose that God employed other than the ordinary secondary means in executing his works of providence. To take just one example, it was the work of the 'third day' that the waters should be gathered together into seas and that the dry land should appear and be covered with vegetation (Gen. 1:9-13). All this according to the theory in question transpired within twenty-four hours. But continents just emerged from under the sea do not become thirsty land as fast as that by the ordinary process of evaporation. And yet according to the principle revealed in Gen. 2:5 the process of evaporation in operation at that time was the ordinary one. (Kline, 151-52)

To put it succinctly: Genesis 2:5 demands that the third day[14] had to be *much* longer than twenty-four hours, for the waters removed early on Day 3 leave the land so parched that it desperately needs rain before the landscape could be clothed with vegetation. Yet a full array of plant life appears at the end of that very day, Day 3 (Ge 1:11). Blocher is confident that "this proof has not been refuted" (Blocher, 56). This surely is the *locus classicus* for the Framework Hypothesis.

Before we begin, we must note several observations that should give one pause before too quickly adopting Kline's innovative exegesis. Our readers should also be aware of further discussion of this matter in Chapter 4 below.

Caution. First, Genesis 2:5-6 is declared by many commentators to be "difficult" (Wenham, 57), "most difficult" (Cassuto, 103), a "perplexing passage" with a significant "ambiguity" of focus (Mathews, 1993). Indeed, Kidner observes that "the difficulty is reflected in the variety of interpretations that have been put forward" (Kidner, "Wet or Dry?, 111). This passage is "widely misunderstood" (Kidner, "Wet or Dry?," 113). Erroneous systems often flow from difficult passages (consider the Mormon theology that derives from 1 Cor. 15:29).

Second, by all accounts Kline's exposition is "new" (Blocher, 53). And this novel exposition does not appear to flow from a dispassionate study of Genesis over the years. Rather, judging from Kline's own writings, it seems to be seeking peace with the assured claims of naturalistic science. His first article introducing his new exegesis shows the heat of controversy in its first sentence, when he refers to "the debate over the chronological data of Genesis 1" (Kline, "Rain," 146). His second to last paragraph concludes: "And surely natural revelation concerning the sequence of developments in the universe as a whole and the sequence of the appearance of the various orders of life on our plant . . . would require the exegete to incline to a not exclusively chronological interpretation of the creation week." His last sentence harkens back to "the primeval ages of creation" (Kline, "Rain," 157).

---

[14] Note Kline's quotations marks around "third day."And observe the Majority Report's wholly inaccurate statement advocates of the traditional exegesis tend to put quotation remarks around references to the biblical days! Majority Report, 5.

Kline's latest article opens with these words: "To rebut the literalist interpretation of the Genesis creation week propounded by the young-earth theorists is a central concern of this article. At the same time, the exegetical evidence adduced also refutes the harmonistic day-age view."[15] The conclusion is that "as far as the time frame is concerned, with respect to both the duration and sequence of events, the scientist is left free of biblical constraints in hypothesizing about cosmic origins" (Kline, "Space and Time," 2). This concept is suggested also in Blocher's frequently referring to traditional exegetes as engaging in "anti-scientism" (Blocher, 22, 48, 224, 227, etc). Erroneous systems often flow from difficult passages — when needed to prove a point.

Third, Kline's exegesis develops a *difficult* passage in a *unique* direction for dealing with a *contemporary* debate. Not only so, but his exposition is set over against superior options — options that are compatible with the traditional exegesis and that do not dismantle the most obvious structuring device of Genesis 1. This may explain why Kline's exegesis is not adopted in the major commentaries. Rather than applying Genesis 2:5-6 to the global scene of Day 3, Keil and Delitzsch (76), Allis (15), Young (61), and others apply the passage to "the place which God prepared for their abode" (Keil, 76) on Day 6. Kidner sees the passage as reflecting Genesis 1:2, stripping the present world of the important vegetation that man will need, while in verse 6 noting the flooding waters over the whole earth (Kidner, "Wet or Dry?"; Sailhammer, 40). Cassuto (102), Hamilton (154), Mathews (193), Sailhammer (40), and others see the fall of Adam anticipated here when these particular plants are introduced (see explanation below).

Fourth, in the final analysis there appears to be some confusion in the Framework camp. A few brief samples of random problems must suffice, due to space constraints.

Ross admits: "The language of the text suggests ordinary providence. Admittedly, the language of the text does not definitively settle the matter, for if Genesis One does teach that creation took place within one week, this language can be reconciled with that view" (Ross, 126).

---

[15] The awkward structure of Kline's sentence casts the rebuttal comment first in order to emphasize it.

Futato expends fully half his entire article in promoting a minority explanation of the *'edh* (אֵד) in Genesis 2:6 as "the crux" of his argument, which he declares plays a "major role" and is a "key to understanding" his Framework exposition. He adopts "rain cloud" (Futato, 5-10; cp. Kline, "Space and Time," 12) over against the almost universally preferred "streams, river, flood"— as originally held by Kline ("Rain," 151; "Genesis," 83) and presently by Blocher (113).[16]

Irons declares that "one who holds to the framework interpretation, then, is not bound to any particular view regarding the age of the earth" (Irons, 3, 6). But then based on his and Kline's comments about the thirsty earth and moving continents, how could they be young earth advocates? The Framework Hypothesis slow providence view will not allow continents to shift so enormously in a one day period. Thus, Kline speaks of the "aeons of creation history" ("Rain," 115).

Interpretation. A view far superior to Kline's is that of Cassuto, Hamilton, Mathews, Sailhammer, Waltke (5:35), and others. Rather than a novel approach to a single verse requiring a re-interpretation of the traditional exegesis of the entire Genesis 1 chapter for the purposes of engaging in a contemporary debate, this verse appears to anticipate the fall of Adam. As Young puts it: "In chapter two events are narrated from the standpoint of emphasis, in preparation for the account of the fall" (Young, 74). Let me explain.

Genesis 1 provides us an account of the creation of "the heavens and the earth" (Ge 1:1). Both the traditional interpretation of creation and the Framework Hypothesis agree that the account of the creation of the universe actually is drawn to an emphatic conclusion with the first three verses of Genesis 2. Note the emphasis on the cessation of creation: "Thus the heavens and the earth were *completed*, and all their hosts. And by the seventh day God *completed* His work which He had done; and He *rested on the seventh day from all His work which He had done.* Then God blessed the seventh day and sanctified it, because in it *He rested from all His work which God had created and made*" (Ge 2:1-3).

---

[16] The great majority of commentaries (e.g., NIV, NRSV, NJPS, NJV, NAB) and scholars agree against Futato. For example, Hamilton declares it: "all but unanimous" (Hamilton, 155). Young says "the translation 'mist' must be abandoned" (Young, 62n). See also, Cassuto, 103; Kidner, "Wet or Dry?"; Mathews, 193; Wenham, 58.

Both the traditional interpretation of creation and the Framework Hypothesis agree that verse 4 serves as a *heading* to what follows: "This is the account of the heavens and the earth when they were created, in the day that the Lord God made earth and heaven."[17] The word "account" (NASB, NIV) or "generations" (KJV, NRSV) is a translation of the Hebrew term *toledoth* (תּוֹלְדֹת). As Kline admits: "In keeping with the uniform meaning of this formula, Gen. 2:4 signifies that what follows recounts not the origins but the subsequent history of the heavens and the earth" (Kline, "Space and Time," 11).

Both the traditional view (e.g., Young, 63; Keil and Delitzsch, 76) and the Framework Hypothesis agree that Genesis 2 "fixes attention . . . on Eden as it sets the stage for the covenant crisis of Genesis 3" (Kline, "Space and Time," 11). Allis even declares of Genesis 2: "the whole second account is, broadly speaking, an expansion or elaboration of Genesis 1. 27. The planting of the garden has nothing to do with 1. 11, 12" (Allis, 15).

Where the conflict between the historic exegesis and the Framework innovation arises is, of course, at Genesis 2:5. The Framework Hypothesis demands that the brief statement here establishes the principle of ordinary providence, which then must govern the entire, lengthy preceding creation account of Genesis 1. This requires that during creation "week" the various geological activities and biological entities are generated by God's fiats, but over an enormous period of time.

The traditional interpretation holds that the fiats of God were supernaturally miraculous in effect, producingf their full blown results immediately The fiat-result refrain shows "the precision and celerity with which the injunction was carried out: as He commanded, and as soon as He commanded" (Cassuto, 26). Of Genesis 1:11 Cassuto states: "On the selfsame day, as soon as the inanimate matter, which serves as a foundation for plant-life, had been set in order, there were created, without delay, the various kinds of vegetation" (Cassuto, 40). When we read in Genesis 1 the declaration "and it was so" we must understand that "it was so instantly, in accordance with God's fiat" (Cassuto, 41). Wenham also notes the "immediate fulfillment of each command" (Wenham, 38). This, of course, comports with a literal six day creative process. It also is reflected in Psalm 33:9: "For He spoke, and it was done; He commanded, and it stood fast."

---

[17] For a careful explanation of verse 4, see Young, 59-60.

Thus, for instance, the geological extrusion of the land surface from beneath the ubiquitous waters transpired immediately rather than gradually. Such action during creation would be similar to the non-providential cosmic miracles of Scripture: for example, the immediate drying up of the Red Sea for the Israelites (Jos 2:9), the incredible halting of the sun on Joshua's "long day" (Jos 10:12), the reversal of the sun for Hezekiah (Isa 38:7ff), and the stilling of the tempest and waves by the Lord (Mt 8:26-27).

How then shall we interpret Genesis 2:5, if it does not establish a providential principle causing us to alter "how we understand everything that has gone before" (Majority Report, 9).

We must begin by observing that in Genesis 2 Moses expressly narrows his focus from "the heavens and the earth, and all their hosts" (2:1) to Eden and its special host, man. Of course as noted above, the Framework Hypothesis agrees with us in this general analysis. But the consequences of this re-orientation and the purpose of 2:5 escape the Framework proponents.

In Genesis 2:4ff Moses begins informing us of what becomes of God's beautiful creation. He opens by pointing out the problem that his audience experiences in creation arises as the result of the actions of his highest created being, man. In Genesis 2:4 God's covenant name Jehovah (*yahweh*, יְהוָה) appears for the first time in Genesis, which along with the unusual word order of 2:4b ("earth and heaven" drawing attention to the earth) and the *toledoth* heading, strongly suggests a change of emphasis.

In Genesis 1 *Elohim* (אֱלֹהִים , translated "God") appears throughout the creation account. *Elohim* acting as "the mighty one" who accomplishes the creation of the entire universe ("the heaven and the earth," 1:1; 2:1, 4) effortlessly by his mere word (eight quick fiats spread over six brief days). But in Genesis 2, rather than emphasizing the powerful creation, Moses emphasizes the covenantal relation: God and man are in covenant, as indicated by Moses' importing the covenant name (Jehovah) into the context of the intimate creative formation of man (2:7; whereas animals were "massed produced," 1:20, 24) and the joyful preparation of a tranquil environment (2:8) with abundant provisions of water (2:6, 10, 13-14), food (2:9 16), peaceful animals (2:19-20) — and a bride for Adam (2:21-24). In all of this beautiful environment there was no shame (2:25) — indeed, all was "very good" (1:31).

Now Genesis 2:5 is placed at the beginning of the *toledoth* of creation, at the head of the account designed to inform us of what becomes of creation. Genesis 2:5 appears in such a way as to anticipate the Fall that soon comes (3:1-24). It informs the reader that he will now learn about the glorious, abundant, loving provision of God for man — conditions that prevailed *before* the reader's well-known circumstances of struggle, frustration, and death. Let us explain.

In Genesis 2:5 Moses speaks to the reader who has just learned that all was "very good" (1:31) and who still has ringing in his ears the sanctifying and blessing of God (2:2-3) on the work he himself accomplished (note the three-fold emphasis on "the work which he had done," 2:2-3). But Moses' audience lives in a wholly different moral and environmental context in the post-Fall world of sin and struggle. Genesis 2:5 informs the readers that *originally* when God readied himself to create man "no shrub of the field was yet in the earth, and no plant of the field had yet sprouted, for the Lord God had not sent rain upon the earth; and there was no man to cultivate the ground."

The "shrub of the field" here is the Hebrew phrase *siah-hassadeh* (שִׂיהַ הַשָּׂדֶה); the "plant of the field" is expressed as *eseb-hassadeh* (הַשָּׂדֶה עֵשֶׂב). As Futato himself so ably demonstrates: "The phrase *siah-hassadeh*, refers to the wild vegetation that grows spontaneously after the onset of the rainy season, and *eseb-hassadeh* refers to cultivated grains" (Futato, 3). This is a rather widely held interpretation found in Cassuto (102), Hamilton (154), Mathews (193), Sailhammer (40), Waltke (5:35), and others. But what does it *mean*? What is its *point*? its revelational *purpose*?

These two types of vegetation are emphasized from within a creation process that highlights vegetation: Day 3 (1:9-13) on which vegetation is created (1:11-12) is emphasized with two fiats (thereby differing from Days 1, 2, 4, and 5). Even the Framework Hypothesis views Day 3 as a climax along these lines, holding that the day on which God creates vegetation (Day 3) corresponds to the day of man's creation (Day 6) (Irons, 30). In fact, when man is created he is specifically given the earth's vegetation for food (Ge 1:29).

Now when we come to Genesis 2:5, we discover that it also emphasizes vegetation and its relation to man and his food supply. To properly grasp its significance we should note that the covenant-making Jehovah God places Adam in a garden with many fruit trees from which he is to eat (2:8-9, 16).

Adam, however, is forbidden access to one particular tree of testing in the midst of all of this lush, abundant, and accesible vegetation (2:9, 17). And as we well know, Adam fails the test by eating from the divinely prohibited vegetation (3:6). Because of this moral rebellion, God curses man in a contextually appropriate and instructive way: God hampers Adam's harvesting of his vegetational food supply which is necessary to sustaining his life (3:17-19, 23) and he cuts him off from the luxurious garden and its "tree of life" (3:22-24). But *still*: What is our point? Where is the Framework Hypothesis error?

Genesis 2:5 focuses on two general classes of plants: the wild scrub brush and the cultivated food grain. Again, as Futato rightly points out: the thorny brush now flourishes in response to rain (Futato, 3, 6, 9); and the grains, such as barley, corn, and wheat, require the cultivating labor of man. *And both of these types of plants are subjects of the divine curse in Genesis 3:17-19.*

Genesis 3:17-19 reads: "Cursed is the ground because of you; in toil you shall eat of it all the days of your life. Both *thorns and thistles* it shall grow for you; and you shall eat *the plants of the field*; by the sweat of your face you shall eat bread, till you return to the field, because from it you were taken; for you are dust, and to dust you shall return." Thus, here we learn that the divine curse causes the field to produce the troublesome "thorns and thistles" and the ground to resist man's production of "plants of the field." The "plants of the field" in 3:18 is the exact phrase found in 2:5 (*eseb-hassadeh* ; עֵשֶׂב הַשָּׂדֶה). The "thorns and thistles" of 3:18 are *synonymous with* and are *specific classes of* the scrub brush (*siah-hassadeh*; שִׂיחַ הַשָּׂדֶה) of 2:5. Many commentaries recognize this relationship between 2:5 and 3:17-19 (e.g., Cassuto, 102; Hamilton, 154; Mathews, 193; Sailhammer, 40; Waltke, 5:35; and others).

Thus, as Moses sets up his account of the moral testing of Adam in Eden he informs his readers *in advance* of the story of the Fall, by taking them back to Day 6 just before the Fall. Though his readers are familiar with laboriously produced fields of cultivated grains and the troublesome scrub brush, it was not always so in God's creation. The grains did not exist in cultivated fields before Adam was created; the bothersome thorns did not infest the ground before Adam's Fall and God's curse. In fact, God's glorious provision for man had him in the garden cultivating it by simply picking the fruit from the trees (Ge 2:15-16), rather than hoeing the resistant ground by back-breaking effort (2:5b). After the Fall he will have to labor by the sweat of his brow against soil hardened "like iron" (Deu 28:23) and as tough as "bronze" (Lev 26:19), so that he may grow the grain that will be necessary to sustain his enfeebled and troubled life. No longer will he eat from the garden trees (2:9, 16), but he "shall eat the plants of the field" (3:18b) by the "sweat of his face" (3:19a).

Consequently, as Moses *opens* his story of man's covenantal testing, he does not look back to the creation process of Day 3, but to the creative result (the Edenic environment of Adam) on Day 6 — and in such a way that anticipates the fateful results of the Fall.

In fact, the Fall is expected in the whole paragraph of Genesis 2:5-9. The record of God's creating Adam from the "dust of the ground" (2:7), anticipates that he will one day "return to the dust of the ground" (3:19) which is the universal experience of Moses' post-Fall readers (Ecc 3:20; 12:7). The presence of the "tree of the knowledge of good and evil" among the other trees in the garden (2:6, 17) anticipates Adam's eating from it (2:17; 3:3), which results in man's return to the dust (3:19) — and also the serpent's curse to "eat the dust" (3:14).

Conclusion. Thus, Genesis 2 is explaining the covenantal test of the well-provided for man. And anticipating his dismal and tragic failure. *This* is the point of Genesis 2:5: God lovingly fashions man and glorioiusly provides for him prior to the scrubs entangling his land and before it is was necessary that he laboriously break the hard clod soil to produce cultivated grains. *After* the Fall futility befalls man's environment (Ro 8:20-23). But it was not always so, according to Genesis 2:5.

Therefore the strained interpretation of the Framework Hypothesis is mistaken. We discover no need to overturn the historic exegesis of Genesis 1 or to reinterpret the confessional position on creation "in the space of six days." The new and unique exposition of one verse cannot sustain the enormous weight placed upon it by Framework theologians. (For further critique of the Genesis 2:5 argument, see Chapter 4 below.)

Two Register Cosmogony as Metaphor Indicator

In that the Majority Report does not deal directly with the Two Register Cosmogony (though Irons declares it as one of three primary exegetical foundations, 27, 36-52), and due to the increasing need to rein in my critique, I will not deal in great detail with this unusual approach to Scripture.

As we are becoming accustomed to expect, we are not surprised to learn that Kline requires an unusual interpretation of Genesis 1:1 to establish his Two Register Cosmogony approach. The "heavens" mentioned in the phrase "the heavens and the earth" is not just a merismus, but represents God's home and the angelic realm ("Space and Time," 4; "Glory," 250). Interestingly, Framework advocate Thompson holds the traditional interpretation, that is, that "the heavens and the earth" simply means the universe (Thompson, 19). Of course, extravagant exegesis is endemic in Kline, who is "not afraid to leave the beaten track" (Blocher, 53). Nowhere do we discover angels or the angelic realm mentioned in the text. Satan's appearing in the guise of a serpent does not require the assumption that the "heavens and the earth" (Ge 1:1; 2:1) also expressly speaks of the angelic Upper Register. For neither do we have an explanation of the fall of Satan, which is also assumed in Genesis 3 without prior textual comment.

From this suppressed premise (the Two Register Cosmogony) in the Majority Report, from this nurturing underground stream flow various interpretive problems. Especially should we note that tainting the argumentative flow are (assumed, but inappropriate) anthropomorphisms which cause our re-interpreting the creation week in light of the hidden Upper Register theology.

Definition of Anthropomorphism. The Framework Hypothesis employs anthropomorphisms in an unusual way. The writers of the Majority Report begin with proper assertions, such as anthropomorphism "describes [God] himself" and "God's actions" and "manner of working" (Majority Report, 8). But Kline ("Space and Time," 9), Irons (46-52), and the Majority Report (p. 8) do not apply anthropomorphism to God, his actions, and his manner of working, but to the *days* structuring creation week. Not only is this hermeneutically inappropriate (Young, 57-58), but as we have asked previously (II. A. 1 and 6): How can earth days be analogies of eternal reality, the "Upper Register," where there is no corresponding succession of moments? There is no "heavenly day"; the concept of "day" is a temporal phenomenon.

Besides, days appear in an appropriate context where time itself begins (Ge 1:1) and in a week wherein the sun was made for the express purpose of marking off days (Ge 1:14, 18). And, once again, if the days represent the Upper Register, the "evening and morning" delimiters only confound the problem by having no point of contact with the eternal order, where there is no evening and morning. As Wenham explains it: "Gen 1 suggests[s] ראשית ["beginning"] refers to the beginning of time itself, not to a particular period within eternity"(Wenham, 14).

What is worse, the Majority Report stands Scripture on its head with this attempt. The Report states: "So we conclude that the creation narrative — specifically the picture of God's completing His creative work in a week of *days* — have [*sic*] been presented in terms of an analogy to a human week of work" (p. 7). But the Fourth Commandment expressly and unambiguously declares the opposite: "Six days you shall labor and do all your work. . . *for* in six days the Lord made the heavens and the earth, the sea and all that is in them, and rested on the seventh day" (Ex 20:9, 11a).

Allegations of Anthropomorphisms. The Framework Hypothesis views Genesis 1 as an anthropomorphic revelation of divine creation. The Majority Report vigorously asserts this in its Section titled: "The Clues That the Passage Must Be Taken Anthropomorphically" (p. 8). The Report notes that "there are many indications in Gen. 1:1-2:3 that God's actions are being described by analogy rather than directly" (p. 8).

Certainly many commentators point to various divine activities recorded in the *second* and *third* chapters of Genesis and suggest that these are "highly anthropomorphic" images (Mathews, 196; cp. Hamilton, 161). For instance, they note that Jehovah's fashioning of man's body from the dust portrays his labor of love in terms expressive of a skillful Potter (2:7a).[18] If this is true, then perhaps Framework advocate Ridderbos is a little closer to the truth than our presbytery's Majority Report. Ridderbos comments on the differences between Genesis 1 and the next two chapters: "In Genesis 2 and 3 the references to God are much more strongly anthropomorphic" (Ridderbos, 27). But even this much-improved observation overstates the matter.

Certainly the more detailed and intimate nature of the revelation in Genesis 2 and 3 is more open to anthropomorphic interpretation. Nevertheless, when analyzed more carefully, true anthropomorphisms are actually absent even here. For instance, though the present participle of the

---

[18] William Dyrness, *Themes in Old Testament Theology* (Downers Grove, Ill.: InterVarsity Press, 1979), 66-67.

verb "formed" (*wayiytser*, וַיִּיצֶר, Ge 2:7) means "potter" (e.g., Jer 18:2), God's activity in Genesis 2:7 is, nevertheless, *realistic history* rather than *anthropomorphic condescension.* In fact, neither party to our presbytery debate proposes that Adam's formation here is really a revelational metaphor signifying simply that God is ultimately his creator, and nothing more. That is, *both* the novel Framework Hypothesis *and* the traditional interpretation agree that Adam's material body was actually fashioned from the dust of the ground by direct, immediate divine action (Kline, "Space and Time," 15 n47; Irons, 72; Majority Report, 36). The more conventional interpretation of creation would argue that Genesis 2:7 records a theophanic activity — just as Kline proposes of Genesis 3:8: "Theophany in human form was evidently a mode of special revelation from the beginning" (Kline, "Genesis," 85).

In fact, Moses does *not* mention anything such as God using his "arms" and "back" in digging up the soil for this special project — though he does speak of God's redemptive activity by using "arm" imagery in Exodus 6:6; 15:16; Deuteronomy 4:34; and 5:15. Nor do we discover a reference to the Lord's "hands" and "fingers" carefully sculpting Adam's body, as in the metaphorical potter imagery in Isaiah 45:9; 64:8; Jeremiah 18:4-6; and Lamentations 4:2. Genesis 2 presents a bold, supernatural event in unadorned, factual form: God formed Adam's body from the ground — without detailing *how* he did it. Thus, anthropomorphism is actually avoided in this revelation of the historical fact of God's creative activity. Furthermore, over against any alleged anthropomorphic imagery in Genesis 2:7 we learn that Adam's body was formed from the dry "*dust* from the ground" — not "clay" as employed in the familiar potter's art in Israel (cf. Isa 29:16; 41:25; 45:9; Jer 18:4, 6). Even Hamilton observes of the verb Moses employs: "'Potter,' however, is a suitable translation only when the context clearly points to the fact that the work of formation being described is that of a potter" (Hamilton, 156).

Furthermore, Irons misinforms his readers when he writes of the Framework Hypothesis that "only the chronological scheme of arranging the creative works of God within six day-frames is figurative" (Irons, 55). This simply is not true regarding what the Framework position asserts. And the Majority Report he helped compose directly contradicts this with numerous (alleged) samples of anthropomorphic figures from Genesis 1 (Majority Report, 8-9). In fact, the Report vigorously declares: "There are *many* indications in Gen. 1:1-2:3 that God's actions are being described by analogy rather than directly" (p. 6; emphasis ours). Note that Irons' "only" becomes the Majority Report's "many." We will quickly refer seriatim to the various *supposed* anthropomorphic expressions drawn from the *first* chapter of Genesis and rebut them.

The Report informs us that: "in the beginning, the Spirit of God is pictured as 'hovering' like a bird over the surface of the waters (Gen. 1:2). But no one supposes that the Spirit actually reined in His omnipresence and developed a locality for the purpose of creating." (Majority Report, 8). Yet Genesis 1:2 does not declare at all that God "reined in His omnipresence." This statement indicates a very important truth of God's relationship to the world: it highlights the *immanence* of God. Though Genesis 1 stresses God's majestic transcendence, whereas Genesis 2 highlights his loving immanence, this statement already prepares us for his immanence in creation. Genesis 1:2 simply points out for the reader that God's Spirit was there — *without localizing him.* After all, is not the Spirit *everywhere* (Ps 139:7)? And if so, then he was *right there*, just as the text states. The Spirit is locally present because everywhere present. As the Puritan Thomas Watson put it: "God's center is everywhere; his circumference nowhere." Genesis 1:2 informs us that the Spirit is actively operating on the scene, which as an aspect of the temporal and material order is necessarily localized. This text is *not* like one that speaks of the "arm" of the Lord, which does not really exist. This is *not* figurative or anthropomorphic imagery, for the Spirit really *does* exist, and he *really was* present over the waters of Genesis 1:2.

As an illustration of this problem, the Report states (also on page 8): "God 'said' things many times during the Creation week. Yet no one supposes He exerted pressure on a diaphragm, vibrated His larynx, and moved air out His mouth while manipulating His tongue and lips." But nowhere does the text state *anything* about God's diaphragm, larynx, tongues, or lips. A problem we have with the Framework advocates is that "their eyes see strange things," as it were. They see things in the text that simply are not there; their *system* requires these things, not the *text*. Certainly Scripture *often* refers anthropomorphically to the "mouth" of the Lord (Deu 8:3; Ps 138:4), his "lips" (Is 33:27), his "breath" (2Sa 22:16; Ps 33:6), and so forth. *But it does not do so in Genesis 1.*

And just as surely, God *does* literally speak in Genesis 1. After all, we read of his literally speaking with Adam alone (Ge 2:16-17) and to Adam and Eve together (Ge 1:28-30; 3:9-19). Do *these* actual conversations imply God has a larynx and lips? *And* Genesis 1 *actually tells us he spoke* (Ge 1:3, 6, 9, 11, 14, etc.) — contrary to the Framework advocates who tell us *he most certainly did not speak*. It is not absurd to assume God speaks to the inanimate world, for we even read of Christ literally speaking to quiet the tempest (Mk 4:39). Furthermore, one glorious difference (among many!) between God and the idols is that the God of Israel speaks, whereas the idols do not (Ps 115:5; 135;16; Dan 5:23; Hab 2:18). Thus, we agree with Young over against the Framework Hypothesis: "The statement, 'and God said,' to take one example, represents a genuine activity upon the part of God, a true and effectual speaking which accomplishes his will" (Young, 56).

The Majority Report also states (again on page 8): "The same logic must be applied when we hear that God 'saw' what He had made and declared it to be good." Why? Is not one of God's names *El Roi*, the "God who sees" (Ge 16:13)? Is not God capable of visualizing the material world he created? And his seeing that "it was good" simply affirms that his creative power brought precisely what he intended.

The text of Genesis *could have* portrayed God as a worker "stretching out his arm" to perform some work (Ex 6:6), extending a "mighty hand" (De 4:34), rolling up his sleeves to get to work (Is 52:10), "stirring up the dust with his feet" (Is 49:23), and so forth. In fact, such anthropomorphic creation-related imagery does appear elsewhere! For instance, Isaiah 40:12 reads: "Who has measured the waters in the hollow of His hand, and marked off the heavens by the span, and calculated the dust of the earth by the measure, and weighed the mountains in a balance, and the hills in a pair of scales?" Such imagery appears in Isaiah 40, Job 38-40, various Psalms, and elsewhere — *but not in Genesis 1.*

Then the Report really stretches the facts (on page 8): "The picture in Genesis 1 is clear. God wakes up. He works until evening. He lies down for the night and repeats the process in the morning. The Spirit has gone out of His way to present the work of God on the analogy of the work of man." Whatever else one might say, no one can assert that this picture presented by the Framework Hypothesis regarding Genesis 1 "is clear." Why has the Church of Jesus Christ missed this "clear" revelation for so long? Nor may you even surmise that "the Spirit has gone out of His way to present the work of God on the analogy of the work of man." *Where* in Genesis 1 do we read anything remotely resembling God waking up, working all day, lying down for the night, and getting up the next day?

The Spirit has *not* "gone out of his way" to present Genesis 1 in these images, the Majority Report has. And that is a big and worrisome difference. Employing Blocher's delicious phrase, we believe that, like Kline, the Majority Report has "left the beaten path" — this time the Scriptures themselves! This is clear evidence that the Framework system requirements are controlling the text, rather than the text controlling the system. And this greatly alarms those of us defending the historic, confessional view of creation.

Neither does the Majority Report fare any better with its allegations of God "resting" on Day 7 — as if that were anthropomorphic (p. 9; cp. Ridderbos, 30; Irons, 67-68). And bringing Exodus 31:17 to bear upon the topic does not help them whatsoever (p. 9; Irons, 68). Two reasons absolutely destroy the Framework Hypothesis argument at this point.

First, the text of Genesis 2:2-3 does not speak anthropomorphically of God "resting," as if relaxing. As I noted previously regarding "The Sabbath Day Problem," Genesis 2 actually informs us that God *"ceased"* his labor (Hamilton, 141-42). As Mathews observes regarding this passage: "The verb translated 'rested' here means 'the *cessation* of creative activity'; it has this same sense in its only other occurrence in Genesis, where God promises the postdiluvian world that the times and seasons 'will never cease' (8:22). Elsewhere we find that God 'rested' (*nûaḥ*, Exod 20:11; *napaš*, 31:17), but here the passage speaks of the absence of work — 'he abstained' from work" (Mathews, 178). That is, God did *not* relax as if from weariness; he simply *ceased* from his creating. Actually the text is even stronger, for as Cassuto puts it: "This verb has been translated or interpreted by many as if it signified 'to rest' or 'to cease work'; but this is incorrect. It has a negative connotation: 'not to do work'" (Cassuto, 63). And most certainly it is literally true that God ceased his creative working. And even though it was not a laborious chore for him, it was most definitely work that effected something — the universe!

Second, importing the imagery of Exodus 31:17 into the debate will not help. The term "refreshed" (וַיִּנָּפַשׁ, *naphash*) in that verse does not appear at all in Genesis 2:2-3. Again, the Framework Hypothesis tends to read into texts things that simply are not there. That God "rested" in the Upper Register (Irons, 51), simply misses the point of Genesis 2:2-3: He "rested," — or better "ceased" — his creative work *in the "Lower Register"* — in time and on earth where his work occurred.

Conclusion. These are a few of my problems with the Framework Hypothesis. Though the Framework Hypothesis is certainly not "without form," it surely is "void."

Chapter 4
THE QUESTION OF GENESIS 2:5
Michael R. Butler

Although Kenneth Gentry has dealt with the Genesis 2:5 in a previous chapter, the text is so important that it deserves some additional consideration. Recognizing that the literary structure of Genesis 1 is not in itself sufficient to establish that the narration of the six days of creation in Genesis 1 is topical and figurative rather than chronological and literal, Framework Hypothesis advocates put forth a supplementary argument based on considerations from Genesis 2:5. Kline is the originator of the argument ("Rain," 146-47), but several others have picked up on it. Futato summarizes it thus:

> The ["Because It Had Not Rained"] article demonstrated that according to Gen 2:5 ordinary providence was God's mode of operation during the days of creation. Since God's mode of operation was ordinary providence, and since, for example, light (Day 1) without luminaries (Day 4) is not ordinary providence, the arrangement of the six days of creation in Genesis 1 must be topical not chronological. (Futato, 1)

Apart from the literary structure argument itself, this is the most frequently appealed to argument in the Framework Hypothesis literature and is considered by some advocates as decisive (Kline "Space and Time," 11-14; Futato, 1; Irons, 31-36; Blocher, 53). In fact, Blocher argues that "this proof has not been refuted" (Blocher, 56). Below I offer a three-fold refutation of the Genesis 2:5 argument. The exegesis fails due to contextual, argumentative, and chronological problems.

Contextual Problems

The most compelling reason to reject Kline's understanding of Genesis 2:5 is that his interpretation is out of accord with the context of Genesis 2:4-3:34 — the context which the *toledoth*-formula of Genesis 2:4 places it. Genesis 2:5 does not have reference to the creation-in-process described in Genesis 1 (Kline's reading), but to the completed creation ready for man to inhabit and subdue. It also anticipates man's probation and fall together with the resultant curse as described in Genesis 3:18. Though man is to be placed in paradise, this soon will be lost when man eats from the forbidden tree. Genesis 2:5-7 anticipates a day when man will no longer enjoy the fruit of the edenic trees created for his nourishment, but must rather labor against the arid ground (fit only for thorns and thistles) in order to cultivate grains by the sweat of his brow. A day in which, because of his sin, he will face physical death and return to the dust from which he was created (cf. Gen. 2:7 and Gen. 3:19b).

Kline's interpretation of Genesis 2:5 is not consistent with the context. He sees that it develops the main theme of Genesis 2 and 3, the theme of man and the vegetation in the garden. But this is quite vague. True, the theme of vegetation and man run throughout Genesis 2 and 3. But the theme is not merely that of vegetation, but specific forms of vegetation – vegetation that characterized the edenic garden and vegetation the characterized the post-curse environment. Moreover, Kline's translation of the Hebrew *ed* as "rain-cloud"[1] (v 6), leaves open the question: Why does Moses give the reason for there being no wild shrubs (that there was no rain) and then immediately add that there went up rain clouds to water the surface of the ground? (see my later argument below).

Perhaps the most problematic aspect of Kline's reading of Genesis 2:5 is that it makes the "because it had not rained" clause out to be nothing more than an *obiter dictum*; a few words thrown in the text that are not germane to the narrative. On this view the reason Moses slipped this clause into the narrative was simply to relay the fact that God did not create vegetation until he had prepared an environment in which it could be sustained by ordinary providence (Kline, "Rain," 149). But contextually, what does this have to do with the Genesis 2 and 3 account? Indeed, such an observation of God's *modus operandi* during the creation week is neither developed, nor referred to nor is connected to anything else in the text. It is just a bit of tangential information.

Futato's, paper, "Because It Had Raided," is primarily an attempt to answer the questions of relevancy that Kline's view invites.

> Why does Gen 2:5 bother to tell us that certain kinds of vegetation were absent *"for the Lord God had not sent rain upon the earth?"* This question

---

[1] Kline here follows the suggestion of Mitchell Dahood in his ""Eblaite *i-du* and Hebrew *ed*, 'Rain-Cloud'," *Catholic Biblical Quarterly* 43 (1981), 534-38. See discussion below for an evaluation of this translation.

has intrigued and perplexed me for some time. Is the absence of rain mere geographical decoration or quasi-irrelevant data that sets the stage for the really important material that follows? Or is this information that is foundational to the narrative and its theology? (Futato, 1)

Futato correctly argues the latter. The information is indeed foundational to the narrative and its theology. However, the particular way in which Futato construes its foundational nature is erroneous.

Futato summarizes his understanding of Genesis 2 as follows:

Gen 2:4-25 is a highly structured topical account with a two-fold focus on *vegetation and humanity*. The two-fold problem of no wild vegetation and no cultivated vegetation (v5), owing to the two-fold reason of no rain and no cultivator (v6), provisionally solved in a two-fold way by the sending of rain clouds and the forming of a man (v7), is roundly resolved in the two-fold synopsis of God planting a garden and putting the man in the garden to cultivate it (v8), and the two-fold expansion with the same focus on *vegetation and humanity* (vv9-25). (Futato 13)

There are at least three problems with this understanding of Genesis 2. First, it is, again, too vague to assert that the two-fold focus of Genesis 2 is vegetation and humanity. Second, Genesis 2:2-7 is not to be understood as a problem-explanation-solution formula. Third, the translation of *ed* as "rain cloud" is unwarranted. I will address these problems in order.

The first problem with Futato's interpretation is that it is too vague to say the twin focal points of the narrative are vegetation and man. It is not vegetation, per se, that is important, but specific kinds of vegetation. Near the beginning of his essay Futato cogently argues that *siah hassadeh* and *eseb hassedeh* are very precise terms. The former means "wild shrubs of the steppe" (Futato, 4) and the latter "cultivated grain." Later in his article, however, he assumes, without any argument or even comment, that the former stands for *all* non-cultivated vegetation. With this new sense of the term in hand he then assumes, again without any argument or comment, that these two types of vegetation (the non-cultivated and cultivated) together stand for all vegetation (Futato 12-13). In other words, he takes it as a given that 'wild shrubs' and 'cultivated grain' are to be understood as a merism for *all* vegetation. But this is certainly not the case.

Genesis 2:8 states that Jehovah God planted a garden and then v 9 records specifically that fruit trees were planted. The garden did not have wild desert shrubs (thorns and thistles) growing in it (what kind of paradise would that be?) nor did it have cultivated grain since man was to eat of the delectable fruit of the trees.[2] The contrast between wild shrubs and cultivated grains (v 5) and resplendent trees bearing choice fruit (v 9) is striking. Clearly, *siah hassadeh* and *eseb hassedeh* do not stand for all vegetation, but a certain type of vegetation; the type of vegetation that would come to characterize the fallen world.[3]

Futato, however, contends that the twin focus on vegetation and man picks up on the theme of Genesis 1, the creation of vegetation and man on the third and sixth days (Futato 14). But notice that on day 3, God creates two types of vegetation (*dese*): "seed-bearing plants" (*eseb mazria zera*) and "trees that bear fruit" (*es perioseh peri*). On day 6 God gives these plants and fruit-bearing trees to man and the animals for food. While the generic term 'vegetation' (*dese*) may imply that all kinds of plants were created, edible as well as non-inedible, it does not imply that that the wild shrubs (*siah hassadeh*), the thorns and thistles mentioned in Genesis 3:18, were part of this creation. The original creation had no scars from the curse. Futato misses the trees for the forest. He recognizes the important themes of man and vegetation, but draws a conclusion that that is much too vague to do the text justice.

---

[2] An interesting sidebar is C. S. Lewis' description of the Perelandran paradise. There the inhabitants eat of the trees laden with fruit and not the cultivated grains produced with the sweat of their brows. Lewis' narration of Ransom's first meal on Venus is poignant. "He had meant to extract the smallest, experimental sip, but the first taste put his caution all to flight. It was, of course, a taste, just as his thirst and hunger had been thirst and hunger. But then it was so different from every other taste that it seemed mere pedantry to call it a taste at all. It was like the discovery of a totally new genus of pleasures, something unheard of among men, out of all reckoning, beyond all covenant. For one draught of this on earth wars would be fought and nations betrayed." C. S. Lewis, *Perelandra* (New York: Scribner, 1996 [1944]), 37.

[3] This conclusion has implications for the understanding of the imperfect *lh* in Gen. 2:6. Both Kline (1958, 151) and Futato (9) understand the term *lh* ("rise up") to be inceptive. Though possible, nothing speaks for it (it is not the expected sense) except for their understanding of the logic of Gen. 2:5-7 together with the assumption that *siah hassadeh* and *eseb hassedeh* refer to all vegetation. Since the latter is erroneous the motivation for this understanding of the verb in this sense is taken away. (See also below for a criticism of Kline's and Futato's logical structuring of Gen. 2:5-7.) That these two considerations taken together are the only two motivations for this understanding is born out by the fact that no modern commentator understands the sense of *lh* to be inceptive. Indeed, Wenham maintains that imperfects in past contexts, such as in Gen. 2:6, express duration. Wenham, 46.

The second difficulty with Futato's understanding of Genesis 2 is the alleged problem-explanation-solution formula he finds there. Below is Futato's argument:

> A coherent picture is emerging: there was no wild vegetation because there was no rain, and there was no cultivated grain because there was no cultivator.
>
> But this point the author has created an expectation in the mind of the reader: the two-fold problem with its two-fold reason will be given a two-fold solution...
>
> Verses 6-7 provide the two-fold solution: "So [God] caused rain clouds to rise up from the earth and watered the whole surface of the ground, and the Lord God formed the man.... Verse 7 says, "The Lord God formed the man...." Here lies the solution to the second prong of the two-fold problem and reason. The logic is cogent and the picture is coherent... This is all rather straight forward and uncontested. (Futato 5)

This approach is hardly uncontested. Apart from Framework Hypothesis advocates, I am not aware of any commentators who take this position. Indeed, many commentators including Cassuto and Hamilton, and to a certain degree Keil and Delitzsch, do not view the absence of certain types of vegetation as a problem to be resolved by rain and human cultivation, but as an anticipation of the cursing of the ground (Cassuto, 100-03; Hamilton, 154; Keil and Delitzsch, 77). As for being straight forward, this interpretation may seem so, but a careful reading of the text proves otherwise. The main problem with Futato's view is that same one that Kline does not resolve: How does this interpretation (the problem-explanation-solution formula) fit into the rest of Genesis 2 and 3?

Futato argues that "Gen 2:4-25 provides an example of the Hebrew stylistic technique of synoptic/resumptive-expansion" where a story is first told in synopsis and then repeated with greater detail (Futato 12). He contends that vv 5-7 are introductory, v 8, the planting of the garden and the making of man, is the synopsis and vv 9-25 are the expansion, with the focus on vegetation and humanity. Thus, Futato's answer to the above question is that vv 5-7 are an integral part of the text because they prepare the way for the synopsis and expansion that constitutes the rest of the chapter.

Apart from the fact that there are no ancient or modern commentators who take this to be the structure of Genesis 2,[4] there are several problems with this reading of the text.

First, Futato finds problems were there are no problems at all. The lack of shrubs (thorns and thistles) and lack of cultivated grain is not a problem to be solved, but rather a description of the world before the fall. This is clear from the context. In Genesis 1:1-2:3 the creation account is given, culminating in man, the image of God. With creation accomplished, Genesis 2:4a introduces a new section that focuses on man and his probation in the garden. Genesis 2:4b begins with the Hebrew expression, "in the day that" which is an idiom for "when." Thus 2:4b reads: "When Jehovah God made the earth and the heavens..." The author is assuming the creation of the earth and heavens has been completed. Indeed, he has just finished narrating the account of the creation in chapter 1. So with the creation in the background he begins to tell the story of man and the fall. Rather than plunging right into the story, though, he begins by giving some background information. The first thing he tells about the finished creation is that there were no wild desert shrubs growing on the earth and no cultivated grain. A reason is given for the absence of both. There were no wild shrubs because God had not sent rain and no cultivated grain because there was man to work the soil. Does this imply that there was no vegetation at this time? This would be a problem since a total lack of vegetation due to a lack of water would conflict with v 4b. That verse, recall, places the time frame of this text after the finished work creation. And part of the finished creation was the vegetation that was given as food for man and animals (day 4). This discrepancy disappears, however, when attention is paid to what the text actually says. The author is not saying that there was no vegetation at this time, but that there an absence of specific kinds of vegetation. The author has previously told us that God created seed-bearing plants and fruit-bearing trees on the 4th day. Here he tells us that there were no wild desert shrubs and cultivated grains. Clearly there is no conflict. There were certain types of vegetation present but not others.

Three questions spring immediately to mind though. First, if there was no rain, how could there be any vegetation? The author provides the answer

---

[4] Wenham, for example, divides Genesis 2 between the creation of man and the garden (vv 5-17) and the creation of woman (vv 18-25). Wenham, 49.

in v 6. At that time there was a spring that came out of the ground that watered the surface of the earth. So while there was no rain, there was an abundant supply of water. The second and third questions are: Why were there no wild shrubs of the field if there was a plenteous supply of water? And why was there no cultivated grain? The answer to the former is obvious. The appearance of wild desert shrubs would be out of place in a land that drank deeply from the plenteous water. Moreover, desert shrubs are not what is expected in a lavish environment of lush vegetation that is described in Genesis 1:11-12. The answer to the latter appears to come in v 7. There the author tells us that man was created from the dust of the ground. Thus it appears that the reason for the lack of cultivated grain was that man was not yet present to cultivate the land.

So far, then, the author tells us of a completed creation. There is a spring coming out of the ground that waters the seed-bearing plants and the fruit-bearing trees and a complete absence of desert-type vegetation. This is a lush environment not a desert environment. Since everything is in place God now creates man, his image-bearer, and places him in this glorious creation that he is to have dominion over. Everything is good. But why does the author bother to mention the fact there was no shrubs and that there was no cultivated grains? The remarks that there were no wild shrubs seems to be merely a piece of trivia while the assertion that there was no cultivated grain seems to be completely superfluous – if there was no man, obviously there was no cultivated plants. That no answer is immediately forthcoming causes the reader to anticipate some sort of explanation. As he reads on he finds the author describing the man being placed in a garden filled with beautiful fruit trees overloaded with delicious fruit. Man is given the task of taking care of the garden and is told by Jehovah God that the fruit is for his nourishment and enjoyment, even the fruit of the tree of life. He is forbidden, however, to eat of the tree of the knowledge of good and evil and if he does eat of it he will die.

Dramatic tension is thus introduced into the story. Everything is good, but there is also a potential for disaster. Paradise may be lost. Light is now shed on the previous statement about the absence of cultivated grains. Man is given the task of tending to the mature garden full of fruit trees. And since he has an abundant supply of food there is no need to cultivate grain crops. But what if man ate the forbidden fruit? Would he still enjoy the lush surroundings of Eden and partake of its choice fruit?

The rest of the story is well known. After Jehovah God made women, she was deceived by the serpent and ate the forbidden fruit. When the man and woman hid in shame, Jehovah God asks, in perhaps the most heartbreaking three words in Scripture, "where are you?" God then curses the serpent, curses the woman and finally pronounces curses upon man. No longer will man enjoy the fruit of the edenic trees. Now he must toil over the recalcitrant soil in order to grow grains that he will make into bread. What was thus anticipated in 2:5-6, and portended in 2:17 has now come to pass. Whereas in the beginning there was no desert shrubs (thorns and thistles), there now will be. Whereas there was no cultivated grains, man will now have to engage in the backbreaking labor of plowing, sowing, irrigating and harvesting them for his sustenance.

But what happened to the spring? The answer is implied by the cursing of the ground. Many commentators suggest that man will now have to contend with the thorns and thistles as though they were weeds choking out his crops. But this is not quite the point (the text certainly does not say this). Rather the land will not be watered as it was before and will thus become arid. From this time forward, the sporadic rain will be its only source of water. Only desert shrubs are fit to grow in such an environment. Thus we can infer that Jehovah God has dried up the spring.

The final curse that is pronounced is that man will die. But notice how this is described. "For dust you are and to dust you will return." (3:19) This takes us again back to the opening section of the narrative where Jehovah God created man from the dust of the ground (v 7). The structure is obvious. What is anticipated in 2:5-7 is consummated in 3:17-19.

Turning back to Futato, on his reading Genesis 2:5-7 has no relationship with Genesis 3:17-19. And since the relationship between the two texts is so obvious, his interpretation of 2:5-7 as a problem-explanation-solution schema must thus be rejected.

Second, Futato's reading of Genesis 2 forces an inexplicable redundancy upon the text. According to Futato, v 5 states a two-fold problem – no wild shrubs and cultivated plants – and a two-the explanation – lack of rain and man. Then in vv 6-7 a two-fold solution is given – rain clouds and man. Then in v 8, the synopsis according to Futato, there is another two-fold solution – Jehovah God planted a garden and placed man in it. But why are there two solutions for each problem? Futato's answer is difficult to understand. He says that vv 6-7 "provisionally solves" the problems of v 5 and v 8 "roundly resolves" them (Futato 13). What he means by this is unclear. He could mean that the sending of the rain clouds was the temporary solution to the problem of the absence of shrubs and that the planting of the garden was the complete or perfect solution. Or he could mean that Moses is structuring his narrative in such a manner that what he writes in v 6 anticipates what he writes in v 8 – what he writes in v 8 completes the thought of v 6. The question is thus: Are the provisional and round resolutions about the world or about the narrative itself? The former seems to be the case since the problems-solutions of vv 5-6 are about the world. The real world problem of there being no shrubs was solved by a real world solution of rain. Consistency, therefore, dictates that we view the second set of solutions as pertaining to the world as well. This implies, however, that the rain clouds that watered the land were only a provisional or temporary solution for the lack of shrubs. But there are two problems with this. (1) On the assumption of ordinary providence, rain is not merely a provisional solution to the absence of shrubs. Rain is always necessary for this type of shrub to grow. (Futato says elsewhere in his paper that rain is the sine qua non of this type of vegetation.) (2) To say that rain was the provisional solution contradicts Futato's interpretation of vv 5-6. The problem was the absence of shrubs and the explanation of this problem was a lack of rain. Thus rain is the complete (round) solution to this problem. Futato's answer, thus, does not solve the problem of the redundancy in the text. This being the case, another interpretation of Genesis 2 should be sought.

Third, Futato's interpretation rests upon inconsistent extensions of the terms *siah hassadeh* and *eseb hassedeh*. As noted above, Futato argues that these terms have very specific meanings ("wild shrubs of the steppe" and "cultivated grain"). This specificity is necessary to make the logic of the problem-solution schema hold up. It is not all non-cultivated plants that need rain (many varieties of trees do not), but the wild shrubs of the steppe do. Moreover, it is not all of the non-wild shrubs of the steppe that need human irrigation (most variety of trees do not), but certainly cultivated grains do. Thus, each specific type of plant is provided for by a specific watering system (rain and irrigation respectively). The logic is indeed tight. The specificity of the plant types and water sources tie the two together. The question now becomes: How can both these two terms which independently refer to specific types of plants, together, in the same context in which their specificity is stressed, represent all forms of vegetation? Notice, the question is not whether the terms can have this or that meaning (individually or together) in any given context, but whether the terms can perform two entirely different functions (have both specific and general referents) at the same time.

The third problem with Futato's view is his understanding of *ed* as "rain-cloud." Before evaluating his arguments for this translation, it should be noted that the word *ed* (which occurs only twice in the Old Testament) is not rendered "rain cloud" in any standard English translation,[5] it is not translated this way in either the Septuagint or Vulgate (both translate the word as "spring") and it is not endorsed by any modern commentary on Genesis.[6] Futato thus bears the burden of proof for his translation.

Futato offers two basic arguments for this translation. First, he refers to Mitchell Dahood's article ("Eblaite *i-du* and Hebrew *ed*, 'Rain Cloud'") in which Dahood argues that *ed* and *i-du* should both be understood as "rain cloud." His reasoning is as follows. The words, *itu* NI-DU ("the month of NI-DU"), appear on an Eblaite calendar as the name of the month that occurs in November-December of our Gregorian calendar, a typically rainy month in Middle East. The same month is called *itu ga-sum* ("the month of heavy rain") in an older Eblaite calendar. Dahood conjectures that because NI-DU refers to the same month as *ga-sum* ("the month of heavy rain") and because the newer calendar on which it appears is more theological in nature than the older one (the names of certain gods become the names of months),[7] NI-DU may be understood to be associated with the celestial source of rain, namely, rain clouds. Dahood also points out that the Eblaite NI-DU may be the cognate of the Sumerian *i-tum* or the Semitic *i-du*. He opts for the latter because it can be identified with the Hebrew *ed*. In the

---

[5] Futato points out that in a footnote for Job 36:27 (the only other place where *ed* occurs in the Old Testament), the NIV translators gives "mist" as an alternative rendering.

[6] Cassuto, 103-104; Kidner, 59; Wenham, 58-59, 156; Nahum M. Sarna, *Genesis*. The JPS Torah Commentary (Philadelphia: The Jewish Publication Society, 1989), 17. Futato does points out that the Targums consistently translated *ed* with the Aramaic word for cloud.

[7] Dahood notes that July-August is referred to as "the month of flocks" on the old calendar, but "the month of Ashtar" (the goddess of fertility) on the new.

two times *ed* occurs in the Old Testament it is associated with rain.[8] Thus every occurrence of NI-DU, which, *ex hypothesis*, is to be understood as the Semitic *i-du*, and *ed* appear in a context which involves rain. And since "rain cloud" makes the most sense out of all three contexts, both should be understood accordingly.[9]

The argument is structured as follows. The meaning of *x* is obscure and the meaning of *y* is obscure. However, the one occurrence of *x* can plausibly mean M and the two occurrences of *y* can plausibly mean M. Term *x* and term *y* can possibly be cognates. If it is hypothesized that they are indeed cognates the evidence for each meaning M is thereby increased. Thus *x* and *y* should be understood as cognates.

Without going into details, note the tenuous nature of this argument. From a formal point of view, the justification of the move from the last premise to the conclusion is obscure. From a material point of view the argument is even thinner. (1) The words in question appear collectively just three times – hardy enough basis to draw strong conclusions from. (2) The calendar-evidence of NI-DU meaning "rain cloud" is inconclusive. (3) Most scholars associate *ed* with either the Akkadian *id* ("cosmic river") or Akkadian *edu* ("outburst of subterranean water") which, as we have seen above, makes much more sense in this context.[10] (4) The identification of

---

[8] Genesis 2:6; Job 36:27. It perhaps occurs as a name in Genesis 36:39, but this is unhelpful in determining the meaning.

[9] Unlike Futato's presentation, both Kline's and Irons' depiction of Dahood's paper are completely inaccurate. Kline states, "These considerations argue in support of the identification of the Hebrew *ed* with the Eblaite *i-du*, 'rain-cloud.'" Kline, "Space and Time," 12. This makes it sound as if the meaning of the Eblaite *i-du*, a word that only appears once in extant sources, was already established! But the meaning of this word, together with its alleged cognate, *ed*, is precisely what Dahood is trying to demonstrate. See Irons, 33, for a repetition of the same error.

[10] In favor of *id* is Cassuto, 104 (he translates it as "waters of the deep"); Sarna, 354, n 8 (he translate the term "flow"); Wenham, 58. Supporters of *edu* include Kidner, 59-60, E. A. Speiser, "'ED in the Story of Creation," in *Oriental and Biblical Studies*, ed. J. J. Finkelstein and M. Greenberg (Philadelphia: University of Pennsylvania, 1967). Hamilton leaves open the possibility of an Eblaite origin, but urges caution. "Given the limited texts that have thus far been published from Ebla, scholars are still reluctant to champion too many connections between Eblaite and Biblical Hebrew." Hamilton, 156.

NI-DU with *i-du* is conjectural.[11] (5) The identification of *i-du* with *ed* is dependent upon the latter meaning "rain cloud." Yet the meaning of *i-du* was supposed to shed light *ed*.

The point here is not to assert that cognate studies should not engage in such tenuous reasoning – the material lends itself to such. However, to take such conjecture and pretend that it sheds great light upon the exegesis of a hotly debated text – the interpretation of which text has great theological ramifications – is a bit disingenuous. Unlike other framework advocates, however, Futato acknowledges as much when he says that his translation of *ed* as "rain cloud" does not depend upon Dahood's argument (Futato 6).[12] Indeed, he contends that whatever the semantic similarities between the *ed* and *i-du*, the biblical evidence can stand on its own (Futato 6).

Futato first offers two reasons why *ed* should not be translated as "stream," what he understands to be the majority view today:[13]

> "Stream" can not possibly be correct for two reasons: 1) The text does not say that the problem was a lack of water in general, a problem which could be solved by water from any one of a variety of sources, for instance, a stream. The problem was a lack of *rain* in particular, because in the ancient Syro-Palestine Levant *rain* was the *sine qua non* of vegetation, especially wild vegetation. 2) "Stream" makes nonsense out of such a well-constructed and tightly argued text. If "stream" is understood, the sense is something like "no wild vegetation had appeared in the land ... for the Lord God had not sent rain ... but a stream was

---

[11] Dahood notes that the scholar who recovered and reconstructed the two Eblaite calendars, G. Pettinato, did not venture a translation of the term. Dahood, 535, n 4.

[12] Actually, the argument that Futato turns to is similar to Dahood's analysis of the biblical texts that contain *ed*.

[13] Futato cites four commentators (Sarna, Scullion, Westermann and Youngblood) as evidence of this. However, Sarna does not, in fact, translate *ed* as "stream" but rather "flow," at term which, in the context of his exegesis, has a different connotation than "stream." "The idea seems to be that the primordial, subterranean waters would rise to the surface to moisten the arid earth... Sarna, 17. "Flow," in this sense is akin to "waters of the deep" (Cassuto), "outburst of subterranean water" (Speiser) and "fresh water ocean" meaning "great spring fed from the subterranean ocean" (Wenham). Thus, "spring" appears to actually be the majority view. Young seems to give hesitant endorsement to "subterranean waters." Young, 150. Even Kline at one time held this view. The word "*ed* probably denotes subterranean waters which rise to the surface and thence as gushing springs or flooding rivers inundate land." Kline, "Rain," 150 n 9.

arising to water the whole surface of the land." If a stream was present to water the whole surface of the land, then there was ample water for the appearance of wild vegetation, and the reason clause ("for the Lord God had not sent rain") is completely irrelevant and illogical. (Futato 5-6)

The first argument fails for at least two reasons. First, this consideration presupposes the problem-explanation-solution formula. But, as has been argued above, v 5 does not state a problem. Rather, it states what the world was like before the curse. Thus v 6 should not be viewed as a solution to this pseudo-problem. Second, Eden was probably located somewhere in Mesopotamia and not the Syro-Palestine Levant. (Moses says Eden was east of Palestine and specifically locates it near the Tigris and Euphrates Rivers.) The principal manner in which much Mesopotamian land was (and is) watered was by river floods not rain. Thus understanding the meaning of the text in light of the Syro-Palestine Levant environment, as Futato does, is misguided. Futato's retort can be anticipated. He would probably argue that Moses is addressing the children of Israel who will be soon be inheriting the promised land (a land located in the arid, Palestine Levant) and, therefore, he (Moses) can best be understood as offering an explanation that would be ecologically relevant to them. Aside from being completely gratuitous, this objection would overlook the obvious. The children of Israel were coming out of Egypt, a land they had been in for 430 years, and Egypt was a land that was (and is) watered by the flooding of the Nile. If Moses had ecological relevancy in mind, then he surely would have spoken of flooding (streams), not rain.

Futato's second argument, is easily answered. Like the first argument, this presupposes the problem-explanation-solution formula of vv 5-7. But the explanation clause is not to be understood as the reason for the "problem" of there not being vegetation in general, but rather as the reason why there was not two *particular kinds* of vegetation – desert shrubs and cultivated grain. These kinds of vegetation were results of the curse.

Futato offers another line of reasoning for translating *ed* as "rain cloud." He argues that Job 36:27, the only other Old Testament passage that the term appears, is best read as: "When he draws up drops from the sea, they distill as rain from his rain cloud (ed).[14]   Given then that *ed* is best

---

[14] This is Dahood's translation. Dahood, 536.

understood as "rain cloud" here, this supports translating *ed* as "rain cloud" in Genesis 2:6.

There are several difficulties with this argument. First, in Job 36:27 *ed* is not rendered as "rain cloud" in any of the major translations.[15] Second, it is not a wise procedure to attempt to understand a relatively clear use of a word (Gen. 2:6 is relatively clear given its context) on the basis of an obscure use of the same word (Job 36:27). Third, the section in which this verse lies is poetic. Being poetry one expects the use of figures and imagery. But Futato's reading of Job 36:27-28 makes it more of a scientific description of the water-cycle than poetry:

> When he draws up drops from the sea, [evaporation and cloud formation]
>
> They distill as rain from his rain cloud. [precipitation from clouds] (Dahood)
>
> The cloud pour down their moisture [precipitation on land]
>
> And abundant showers fall on mankind. (NIV)

In keeping with the poetic nature of Job, Kline offers a better interpretation of the passage:

> The word [*ed*] appears elsewhere in the Old Testament only in Job 36:27. That passage is also difficult; but [*le edo*] there seems to denote the underground ore, as it were, from which the raindrops are extracted and refined, *i.e.*, by the process of evaporation in the cycle of cloud formation and precipitation (Kline, "Rain," 150, n 9.).

On this rendering, Elihu is exalting God for his provision of rain and he describes this provision, which he understands is based upon the known water-cycle, in poetic terms.

With this, Futato's positive case for rendering *ed* as "rain cloud" is unpersuasive. More, however, can be said against Futato's view.

First, Genesis 2:6 states that, "an *ed* came up from the earth."[16] But since rain clouds do not come out of the earth, this tells against translating *ed* as "rain cloud." Futato retorts that Moses is speaking phenomenologically; it appears to the observer that rain clouds come up

---

[15] As mentioned above, the NIV translators gives "mist" as an alternative rendering.

[16] Cassuto (104), Hamilton (150) understand 'earth' (*eres*) as 'underworld'. A rendering that, "enjoys growing assent from Hebraists" according to Hamilton.

from the earth (Futato 8). Though it is true that the Bible does describe clouds as coming up from the earth (Ps. 135:17; Jer. 10:13; 51:16), all these descriptions occur within poetry. Genesis 2:6 is clearly not poetry. Note also that that in each of the poetic accounts that use the language of appearance, the rain is not said to come out of the earth, but out of the *ends* of the earth.[17] Furthermore, given that there is no positive reason to accept Futato's translation of *ed* as "rain cloud," there is nothing in the text that leads us to conclude that Moses is using the language of appearance to describe the rising of clouds.

Second, Futato's translation conflicts with Genesis 2:10 which clearly states that the garden was watered by a river. Futato's response is strained. Following Cassuto he contends, correctly, that "the repetition of the hiphil of *sqh* in v 6 and v 10 is part of an argument for taking *ed* as a reference to the river of v 10" (Futato 9).[18] He then implausibly adds, "The repetition, however, can be explained as a means of connecting the source ("rain clouds;" v 6) with the result ("river," v 10)." Apart from the fact that this is quite a stretch, this interpretation does not even make sense on his own terms. According to Futato, v 6 tells us that it was rain clouds that watered the surface of the earth. Verse 10 tells us that rivers were what waters the earth. Futato reconciles these verses by asserting that rain clouds are the *source* of rivers. The picture is that the rain falls, the river swells, the land is watered by the river. But notice that Futato elsewhere argues that rain not rivers or streams is the sine qua non of vegetation in the Syro-Palestine Levant (Futato 5). In other words, according to Futato, streams *cannot* be what watered the earth.

Futato's next move is truly remarkable. He writes, "But even if *ed* is defined by the "river," the presence of rain simply becomes an unargued presupposition of the text" (Futato 9). After pointing out that ancients understood the nature of the rain-cycle he continues, "Since such rivers are fed by rain...the presence of a *nhr* [perennial river] would be proof of the presence of rain rather than an objection to it." In other words, because ancients as well as moderns understand where river water comes from, the

---

[17] Futato also cites 1 Kings 18:44 (Elijah's servant said a "cloud as small as a man's hand is rising from the sea") as corroborating evidence.

[18] See also Cassuto, 104.

interpreter is forced to acknowledge that rain was present. Futato *assumes* ordinary providence (ordinary in our experience after the fall) during the pre-fall state. Apart from being an assumption, not an argument, these comments indicate that Futato does not even consider the possibility that Jehovah-God may have preserved his creation in a different manner than he does now. This, perhaps more than anything else, illustrates the danger of allowing uniformitarian assumptions to control the interpretation of the Genesis text.[19]

A plain reading of the text, however, leads one to understand that Eden was not exactly like the cursed world today.[20] We lost something real. Reformed theologians concentrate on the loss of man's original righteousness. And well they should. But let us not forget that many other things accompanied this loss. There was no death or decay, animals behaved differently towards man then, man walked about unclad and unashamed, man ate the fruit of the trees and did not toil over the sowing and harvesting of grain crops. The world is not like this anymore. Paradise has been lost.[21] To view the curse in completely spiritual terms is alien to

---

[19] This, by the way, sheds light on why the very first conclusion that Futato says he will demonstrate in his article is that it rained before the flood. At first, this seems to be a curious statement. Why bother to mention it? The answer is that Futato is making a dig at creation scientists who say that the Noahic flood waters come from waters in the expanse. Those who hold such a view clearly reject uniformitarian assumptions. It appears that Futato believes such "pseudo-science" to be an embarrassment to the church. If God did not work exactly the same way today as he did at the time of creation (sequence and duration of the days of Genesis aside) scientists are not free from biblical constraints to hypothesize about cosmic origins. The only way scientists may investigate the history of the earth and universe is on the assumption that the past is like the present. An interpretation of Genesis 2 that allowed for a different mode of ordinary providence is, thus, unacceptable. Whether creation scientists are right or wrong about there being no rain before the flood is beside the point. What is the point is that it appears that something other than textual considerations are being introduced in the interpretation of the biblical text.

[20] This statement *does not* imply that it was completely different either.

[21] The utter splendor of Eden is difficult for even redeemed men to imagine let alone describe. Milton perhaps came closest but, alas, even he only just penetrates the rind:

> Under a tuft of shade that on a green
> Stood whispering soft, by a fresh Fountain side
> They sat them down, and after no more toil
> Of thir sweet Gard'ning labor than suffic'd
> To recommend cool *Zepher*, and made ease

Scripture. The assumption of uniformitarianism therefore is completely alien to the text. Take away this assumption and the conclusion one draws is obvious: the manner in which Jehovah God watered the surface of the ground was different in Eden.

Third, if the problem was, as Futato maintains, a lack of rain (*matar*), why does Moses say, again on Futato's view, that the Jehovah God sent rain clouds (*ed*)? One expects that he would use the same word both times.

Fourth, Futato's argument depends on the terms "shrubs of the field" and "cultivated grain" standing for all vegetation. If this is not correct (as has been argued above), this would render the translation of *ed* as "rain cloud" impossible. The reason is obvious. If Moses is speaking of specific types of vegetation that were not on the earth and gives the reason for there not being there as a lack of rain, this implies the vegetation that was there was watered by some other means.

Fifth, Genesis 13:10 provides external evidence that *ed* is not be understood as "rain cloud": "Lot looked up and saw that the whole plain of the Jordan was well watered, like the garden of the Lord, like the land of Egypt, toward Zoar." Why did Lot compare the plain of Jordan to Eden and the land of Egypt? Wenham provides the answer: "Powerful springs in the Jordan valley and beside the Dead Sea create very fertile areas, e.g., at Jericho, Ain Feshka, and Engedi. According to Genesis, the whole area was much more fertile before the destruction of Sodom and Gomorrah (cf. Chap. 19)" (Wenham 297). As for Egypt, the flooding Nile brought great fecundity to the land. The point, therefore, is not merely that the plain of the Jordan is fertile just like Egypt and Eden, but rather, they are fertile in the same kind of way. To borrow a phrase from Kline, the unargued

---

More easy, wholesome thirst and appetite
More grateful, to thir Supper Fruits they fell,
Nectarine Fruits which the compliant boughs
Yielded them, side-long as they sat recline
On the soft downy Bank damaskt with flow'rs:
The savory pulp they chew, and in the rind
Still as they thirsted scoop the brimming stream

Paradise Lost, Book IV, 325-336.

The only consolation we have for the paradise lost is the even greater paradise we gain in Christ.

presupposition of the text is that Eden, like Egypt and the plain of the Jordan, is watered by streams not rain clouds.

Sixth, Psalm 104:10, which is a reflection of God's work of creation, teaches that God watered his creation with springs (Weeks 101).

Seventh, there is a biblico-theological reason not to adopt the "rain cloud" translation. A passage from Kline's *Images of the Spirit*, sets up the argument nicely:

> Decorative features of the temple included carvings of flowers, palm trees, and cherubim and in the eschatological sanctuary are found *the river and trees of life*. In Ezekiel 47 the same verb is used as in Genesis 2 for the issuing forth of the river, which in both passages flows on a *fructifying* course eastward. Ezekiel sees the river emerging from under the lintel of the temple entrance, which ... was a reflex in the temple's architectural symbolism of the Glory-cloud, whose mountain throne-site in Eden was evidently the *spring-source of the river of paradise* (Kline, "Images," 41-42; emphasis mine MRB).

Notice that Kline says the edenic trees were watered by a river that has a spring-source and not a rain-source.[22] This is precisely what Ezekiel 47 describes – a passage that Kline correctly sees as parallel to Genesis 2. There, Ezekiel says waters spring forth from the temple (v 1) which, in turn, become the source of an overabundant river (v 5). This river, in turn, waters fruit-laden and healing trees on either bank (v 12).[23] This imagery is picked up in Revelation 22:1-2 which identifies the source of the heavenly river as the throne of God.[24] The point is that these parallel passages all speak of a river that has its source in a spring (literal or figurative) and not in rain-clouds. Using the analogy of Scripture, the way to understand *ed* is not as a rain cloud, but as a spring. Furthermore, since Ezekiel makes reference to Eden and Revelation makes reference to Ezekiel, to interpret *ed* as "rain cloud" would be tantamount to saying that Ezekiel and the Apostle John misinterpreted Scripture for clearly they believed that Eden's water was supplied by a spring and not rain clouds.

---

[22] To contend that rain is the source of the spring would be quite a stretch. Indeed, in many cases it would not be true.

[23] Objection: "But the these trees are healing, unlike the trees of Eden." Answer: There was no need of healing in Eden. The leaves of these trees are to heal the effects of the curse (Rev. 22:3).

[24] Jesus says that from him swell fountains of everlasting life (John 4:14; 7:36-39).

On the basis of all of the above reasons, *ed* is not be understood as "rain cloud." Futato's interpretation of Genesis 2:5-6 ("No wild vegetation had appeared in the land … for the Lord God had not sent rain … so God sent rain") (Futato 6) is thus not correct. The text is more accurately paraphrased: "At that earlier time before the fall and curse, no thorns and thistles had appeared in the land … for the Lord God had not sent rain … but God at that time watered the earth with springs from the deep."[25]

Two questions immediately come to mind given this paraphrase. First, does this interpretation mean that rain is a curse? Not at all. Rainfall is like the clothing God made for the man and woman. That Adam and Eve needed clothing was a result of sin. That God provided them with clothing was a blessing. Likewise, that the land needed rain was a curse, that God provided rain was (and continues to be) a blessing.

Second, does this interpretation imply that there was no rain before the curse? Not necessarily. The occurrence of rainfall cannot be inferred either way from the text. The point of the "because it had not rained clause" is that the normal way of watering the garden before the fall was by ceaseless streams of water welling up from springs. The land enjoyed a constant supply of water and was not dependent upon fickle rain.[26] After the fall God cursed the ground. It should be obvious that the principle manner in which ground is cursed is by removing its water supply.[27] Deserts are the

---

[25] This paraphrase fits nicely with the NIV's translation of Gen. 2:4b-7a: "When the Lord God made the earth and the heavens – and no shrub of the field had yet appeared on the earth and no plant of the field had yet sprung up, for the Lord God had not sent rain on the earth and there was no man to work the ground, but stream came up from the earth and watered the whole surface of the ground – the Lord God formed the man …" It is peculiar that Kline does not interact with this common interpretation. Not only does Cassuto hold the anticipatory interpretation of Genesis 2:5, Hamilton (154) and Stigers do also. H. G. Stigers, *A Commentary on Genesis* (Grand Rapids: Zondervan, 1976, 65). Of this omission Jordan comments, "This is not good scholarship." James B. Jordan, *Creation in Six Days: A Defense of the Traditional Reading of Genesis One* (Moscow, Idaho: Canon Press, 1999), 57. Futato cites Cassuto on the occurrence of "cultivated grain" in Genesis 2:5 and 3:18, but does not interact with Cassuto's main argument. Futato, 4 n. 10.

[26] Fickle from a human perspective. Note that unlike fountains or springs which are unexceptionally viewed as a blessing in biblical imagery, rain is viewed as both a curse (e.g. Gen. 7:12; Exod. 9:13-35; Sam. 12:17-18) and a blessing (Deut. 28:12). Conversely, the lack of rain is often viewed as a curse.

[27] Biblical imagery often associates water with blessing and desert wastes with a curse.

most cursed of all lands; they are extremely toilsome to cultivate. Thus after the fall, man would be dependent upon rain or irrigation to water the land.

In conclusion, then, Futato's three arguments for his interpretation of Genesis 2 prove abortive. Thus while Futato's reading of Genesis 2 brings some structure to the text that Kline's does not, it ultimately cannot rescue Kline. 27 If Futato's understanding of the structure is erroneous, then the conclusion he draws regarding the dis-chronology of Genesis 1 does not follow. He argues that (1) since Genesis 2 has as a problem-explanation-solution formula which (2) introduces a thematically structured narrative (vegetation and man) that is not arranged chronologically and (3) since Genesis 1 also has a problem-solution formula (the earth being "unproductive and uninhabited" and "darkness" is viewed as the problem and the creation of inhabitants and luminaries as the solution) and (4) it (Genesis 1) is structured thematically around vegetation and man, the conclusion to be drawn is that Genesis 1 must be topical rather than chronological. Notice that if one premise is false, the whole argument falls apart. It has been shown that (1) is indeed false, but the other premises are also questionable. While premise (2) is acceptable, though not necessary, on the account above, many have argued against understanding Genesis 2 as non-chronological. See, for example, Joseph A. Pipa, Jr., "From Chaos to Cosmos: A Critique of the Non-Literal Interpretations of Genesis 1:1-2:3" in *Did God Create in Six Days?*, Joseph A. Pipa, Jr. and David W. Hall, eds. (Taylors, SC: Southern Presbyterian Press, 1999), 154ff.

As for (3), there are at least two problems. First, Futato's premise is based on his adoption of a minority reading of *tohu wabohu*. Second, even if Genesis 1 does contain a problem-solution structuring, there are too many literary differences with Gen. 2:5 to allow them be viewed as parallels. For example, whereas Genesis 2 gives an "explanation" for the two "problems" (no rain, no man), Genesis 1 does not. On Futato's reading there is really a three-fold problem (an unproductive, uninhabited and dark world) not a two-fold problem as Gen 2:5, as his interpretation, portrays. Thus there is a lack of symmetry that one would expect. Finally, the manner in which the author supposedly gives the solutions to the problems differs radically. Genesis 2 "solves" the "problems" of v 5 in two verses (6-7), but Genesis 1 "solves" the "problems" in 29 verses. Premise (4) is also highly debatable. Many commentators deny Genesis is thematically structured (e.g. Young). But even granting that Genesis 1 is thematically structured, most commentators do not see the creation of vegetation and man as the two major themes. Every one of Futato's premises is, thus, open to serious criticism.

Notice further that even if all four premises were true, Futato's conclusion would still not necessarily follow. All he has shown is that the problem-solution schematization indicates thematic development that is not necessarily chronological in nature. He has not demonstrated that thematic development rules out chronological development. At best he can assert that thematic development should cause the reader not to anticipate chronological development. So granting Futato his four premises, we should, perhaps, not take Genesis 1 as chronological all things being equal. But all things are not equal. Given the text's emphasis on chronology (the "evening and morning" refrain, use of yom, use of ordinals, numbered sequence, etc.) these premises are not be enough to justify a non-sequential reading of the text.

One last comment on Futato's paper is in order. He believes his reading of Genesis 1 and 2 has implications for understanding the theology of the text. Specifically, the reason this text is concerned with vegetation and rain is that it was a warning to Israel not to go after Baal, the storm god of the Canaanites who brought rain (hence vegetation) to the arid land. Simply stated, God styled the creation account as a polemic against Baalism. Much could be said against this, but two comments will suffice. First, this assumes that the Hebrews did not know the creation account before the time of Moses (the only time an anti-Baalism polemic would be relevant). This is hardly possible. Certainly Moses' ancestors such as Abraham and Noah would have known what we call the Genesis 1-3 creation-fall account. Second, Moses himself would not have known enough about Baalism to write about it. He was never in Palestine nor would he have been trained in Canaanite theology (he learned Egyptian theology, cf. Acts 7:22).

But unlike Kline's non-integrated view and Futato's mistaken view of Genesis 2, the interpretation presented herein shows that far from being an extraneous bit of trivia, the explanation for the lack of certain type of vegetation is beautifully woven into the thematic tapestry of chapters 2 and 3 where the fall and the resultant curse change the means of harvesting from picking fruit off of the trees to back-breaking sowing and reaping of crops.

Before this section is concluded, one more issue needs to be addressed. Kline contends that, details aside, any interpretation of Genesis 2:5 has implications for Genesis 1. That is, Genesis 2:5 presupposes, on any reading of the text, ordinary providence during the creation week: "The simple, incontestable fact [is] that Gen. 2:5 gives an explanation, a perfectly natural explanation, for the absence of vegetation somewhere within the creation 'week'" (Kline, "Space and Time," 13). But this is just not the case. Given the interpretation defended above, Genesis 2:5 anticipates the fall and curse rather than recapitulates an aspect of the creation in Genesis 1. Genesis 2:5 refers to the time after the fall when man would have to contend with wild shrubs (thorns and thistles) in the cultivation of grain. No longer would the ground be watered by springs (vv. 6, 10), but by rain and irrigation. Thus, far from presupposing ordinary providence was operating during the creation period (Kline, 149-50), Genesis 2:5 tells us almost the exact opposite.

The edenic environment was quite different from the post-lapsarian environment. The curse brought with it changes in ordinary providence. Pain, death and decay came not only to man but the entire creation.[28] Much of what was ordinary in Eden would be extraordinary today. And vice versa. So Calvin:

> But although he has before related that the herbs were created on the third day, yet it is not without reason that here again mention is made of them, *in order that we may know that they were then produced, preserved, and propagated, in a manner different from that which we perceive at the present day....* But, at that time, the method was different:... [Vegetation] possessed durable vigour, so that they might stand by the force of their own nature, and not be the quickening influence which is now perceived, *not by the help of rain ... but by the vapour with which God watered the earth.*[29]

Argumentative Problems

Even assuming that Kline's interpretation of Genesis 2:5 is correct all this proves is that ordinary providence was operative during the creation

---

[28] See John Murray, *The Epistle to the Romans* (NICNT) (Grand Rapids: Eerdmans, 1968), 1:299-310.

[29] John Calvin, *Commentaries on the Book of Genesis*, vol. I, John King, trans. (Grand Rapids: Eerdmans, 1948), 110-111.

week. But to draw from the fact that ordinary providence was operative during the creation week, a fact that traditionalists readily acknowledge even apart from the Genesis 2:5 argument, the conclusion that *only* ordinary providence (aside from creative acts) was operative is a non sequitur.[30] Not only does this conclusion not necessarily follow, there are reasons to believe the conclusion does not even follow with a modest degree of probability. Ordinary providence has prevailed since the creation week and yet God has repeatedly worked without, above and against ordinary means. If God does not limit himself to works of ordinary providence during this era of completed creation, it is gratuitous to say he limits himself to it in the period of creation. Indeed, given the framework interpretation's view that God created over a long period of time and thus earlier eras lacked much of the finishing touches of creation, it is difficult to imagine just what ordinary providence would amount to in such an environment.

Chronological Problems

There is a contextual indication that extraordinary providence was operative during the creation week irrespective of one's interpretation of the six creation days. After describing the initial creation of the heavens and earth, Genesis 1:2 states "the Spirit of God was hovering over the waters." Though this is a notoriously difficult text, it does seem to at least signify that the Spirit was protectively looking over the new creation in the same way an eagle protectively hovers over its young.[31] The infant creation is not able to take care of itself and so God provides supernatural preservation. Hamilton's comment is apposite: "Yes, there is a formlessness there, a forboding darkness, but all is kept in check and under control by the spirit of God" (Hamilton 115). Supernatural protection is thus present from the

---

[30] See Pipa, 163-4.

[31] Deuteronomy 32:11. This is the only other occurrence of the term *merahepet* ('hover') in the Old Testament. Cassuto explains the parallel senses between these two texts. "Just as the eaglets, which are not yet capable of fending for themselves, are unable by their own efforts to subsist and grow strong and become fully-grown eagles, and only the care of their parents, who hover over them, enables them to survive and develop, so, too, in the case of the earth, which was still and unformed, lifeless mass, the paternal care of the Divine Spirit, which hovered over it, assured its future evolution and life." Cassuto, 25. See also Pipa, 164.

very beginning. This being the case, there is every reason to expect supernatural providence to continue throughout the creation week.

Because of the conjecture that ordinary providence was the *modus operandi* of the creation "week" described in Genesis 1, Framework Hypothesis advocates must at least hold to the following basic sequence of creation: (1) The light and luminaries as well as the seas, land and atmosphere were created before the plants, animals and man. (2) The luminaries must have been created before sea and land and the atmosphere for otherwise, according to Kline, "earth would have come into existence by itself as a solitary sphere, not as part of the cosmological process by which stars and their satellites originate, and it would have continued alone, suspended in a spatial void (if we may so speak) for the first three "days" of creation" (Kline, "Space and Time"). (3) Vegetation must have been created prior to the animals and man since vegetation provides sustenance for them.

With at least this much settled, the question may be asked, when does the situation described in Genesis 2:5 (on Kline's interpretation) occur in the order of creation? There are only three basic scenarios possible:

Scenario One[32]	Scenario Two	Scenario Three
Light and luminaries	Light and luminaries	Light and luminaries
Atmosphere	Sea and land	Sea and land
Sea and land	Atmosphere	Situation of Genesis 2:5
Situation of Genesis 2:5	Situation of Genesis 2:5	Atmosphere

Upon close scrutiny, however, it turns out that none of these scenarios are possible due to either ordinary providence or interpretive considerations.

Scenario One turns out to be impossible given the principle of ordinary providence. Since the sun would have evaporated some of the water into the atmosphere, precipitation would have naturally occurred almost immediately. Thus rain would have fallen before the separation of the land

---

[32] Each scenario is temporally ordered from top to bottom.

from the sea.[33] But because rain would have fallen, there would have been vegetation on the earth since the reason given in Genesis 2:5 for there not being vegetation (according to Kline's interpretation) was because it had not rained. This results in vegetation being created before land! Clearly this situation would necessitate extraordinary providence.

Scenario Two avoids the problems of Scenario One. But notice that once the atmosphere was created, ordinary providence would bring about precipitation almost immediately (the sun would evaporate the waters which would cause rain clouds and thus rain). This results in forcing the situation described in Genesis 2:5 (according to the Framework Hypothesis) – where there is said to be no vegetation on the land because it had not rained – to be wedged into a very short time-frame. But if this were the case, if there was only a very short time between rain and the creation of vegetation, why would Moses bother to mention it? Kline's own argument against the traditional view is pertinent:

> [On the literalists' interpretation of Genesis 1] the absence of vegetation or anything else at any given point would not last long enough to occasion special consideration of the reasons for it. Within that time-frame such a question would be practically irrelevant. (Kline, "Space and Time,"13)

Thus, Scenario Two fails.

Scenario Three avoids the problems of the other two scenarios. It does not have vegetation appearing before the creation of land (as per Scenario One) nor does it preclude "an environmental situation that has lasted for a while" (as per Scenario Two). Thus on these scores this account makes sense of the Framework Hypothesis' interpretation of Genesis 2:5. But what it gains in consistency it looses in plausibility.

Scenario Three lacks plausibility for at least two reasons. First, it makes a gratuitous assumption about the environmental condition that pertained in Genesis 2:5. The only reason someone would infer from this text that there was no atmosphere at the time the situation described therein pertained would be to try to save his theory. One reads it and just assumes there was an atmosphere. Indeed, it seems to describe a situation very much

---

[33] A Framework Hypothesis advocate could maintain that the sea and land were separated with a very short time after the creation of the atmosphere. But this goes against the "era-perspective" of Genesis 2:5, a text that "assumes a far more leisurely pace on the part of the Creator, for whom a thousand years are as one day." Kline, 13.

like our own – land, sea, air – with the notable exception that there was no rain.[34] Second, it would be extraordinarily odd for Moses to explain that the absence of vegetation on the land was due to the absence of rain in the context of an environment where there was no atmosphere! (This would be like latecomer to Presbytery who explained that he was tardy because his car broke-down on the way, when, in fact, the reason for his car breaking down was that he was in a head-on collision with another vehicle.) The lack of rain in such a situation would not be the most notable or pertinent or interesting explanation for the absence of vegetation. The antecedent explanation for there being no rain, namely, that God had not yet created the atmosphere, would be far more noteworthy. The Third Option forces a strained and bizarre understanding of the situation described in Genesis 2:5 and should therefore be rejected.

Because the three options above are the only three possible options and because none of the three options is viable, the interpretation of Genesis 2:5 given by defenders of the Framework Hypothesis is likewise not viable. This being the case, framework advocates cannot read back into Genesis 1 the principle of ordinary providence. And given that the sole exegetical reason for denying extraordinary providence in Genesis 1 proves faulty, there is no reason to interpret the six days of creation as anything but sequential 24-hour days on the basis that such sequence and duration would necessitate extraordinary providence.

Creation Product Conflation. Proponents of the framework interpretation not only conflate the sequence of the creation of light (Day 1) and the creation of luminaries (Day 4), but the products of creation as well. This is implied by the simple fact that, on the principle of ordinary providence, the sun, by its very nature, puts forth light. It is not an extraordinary working of providence that the sun shines every day. It has been endowed with this property much like copper has been endowed with the property of efficiently conducting electricity. Thus to assert that God created light and yet simultaneously in a distinct act created the sun would be a violation of the principle of ordinary providence. This entails that the six "days" of Genesis 1 are comprised of seven rather than eight creative

---

[34] Of this verse Sarna comments, "The existence of both celestial and subterranean stores of water are presupposed here [Gen. 2:5]." Sarna, 17. Sarna understands the expanse to be celestial water whereas framework advocates understand it as atmosphere.

acts. This implication of the "ordinary providence" argument is made explicit by Futato: "… the accounts of God's work on Days 1 and 4 are *two different perspectives on the same creative work*" (Futato 16; emphasis MRB). Kline is in agreement. "In terms of chronology, day four thus brings us back to where we were in day one, and in fact takes us behind the effects described there to the astral apparatus that accounts for them" (Kline, "Space and Time," 8). If the luminaries (the astral apparatus) are the causes of daylight and the day/night cycle (the effects Kline refers to), then there would be no need to create, in a completely distinct act, daylight and the day/night cycle. If the *cause* is in place, the *effects* follow in due course. Effects are not created in separate events. To assert otherwise would be to violate the ordinary providence principle.[35]

This trimming of the number of creative events during the creation week has serious theological consequences for the framework interpretation; consequences that its advocates such as Irons are anxious to deny.

> Orthodox defenders of the framework interpretation strenuously assert that God's creative work must be defined as a series *of at least eight supernatural acts of origination*. The creative acts of Gen. 1 transcend ordinary providence. They are supernatural events. They are creative events. Although providential governance was in effect after the initial *ex nihilo* creative act (Gen. 1:1), the subsequent creative acts, as represented by the eight fiat-fulfillments, must be viewed as acts of creation supernaturally interrupting the course of ordinary providence. (Irons 73; emphasis MRB).

Irons specifically argues that while the creative acts of days 1 and 4 were contemporaneous, they were nevertheless distinct and that the luminaries are the physical mechanisms employed to *sustain* light (Irons 58, 59). In other words, God simultaneously in two separate acts created light and the light bearers.[36]

---

[35] To deny this would also be absurd. God created lightning (or at least the conditions that produce lightning), but he did not create thunder in a separate act. Lightning causes thunder.

[36] The irony of this position is that framework advocates castigate the literal interpretation for having the sun created three days after light, a clear violation of ordinary providence. And yet they argue that light and the sun were created in separate fiats.

But what does Iron's mean by asserting that the luminaries sustain light? Notice that this is an odd word to choose. One does not typically say that the sun sustains light any more than one says that fire sustains heat or that clouds sustain rain. English speakers typically say that the sun causes light or is the source of light, or simply, the sun shines. Elsewhere Irons himself follow our common linguistic convention:

> The fact that the sun was the *source* of daylight is not a recent discovery of modern science. Ancient Hebrews were aware of this obvious relationship through simple observation (Irons 31; emphasis MRB).

Given such customary expressions, why would Irons choose to use the unconventional word 'sustain' in the context referred to above? The answer becomes obvious when one recognizes that Irons and other framework advocates are faced with the following dilemma. One the one hand, Irons does not want to say that the sun causes light, otherwise there is no need of a separate creation of light. On the other hand, he does not wish to say that there is no causal relationship between the sun and light since this would violate ordinary providence. So how does he avoid this dilemma?[37] He uses a neutral verb that does not commit him either way. But note that 'sustain' in this context has no particular meaning and its use only obfuscates the issue. Once clarity is sought, framework advocates will have to say one or the other.

The ordinary providence argument therefore leads us to conclude that there are only seven creative events during the creation week. This result is serious enough, but this reduction of the number of fiats leads to even greater problems. If the creative acts of day 1 and day 4 are really the same act, if they are "two different perspectives on the same creative work," then perhaps other creative acts can be conflated as well. There certainly would be nothing to rule out this possibility a priori. Indeed, if this were the case, one should rather expect this to be true of other acts of creation.

Could not day 5 be a temporal recapitulation of day 2? Especially given Kline's view that day 2 like day 1 focuses on a realm (the expanse and seas) while day 5 like day 4 focuses on the ruler or inhabitant of that realm (birds and sea creatures). Given this parallelism and given that Genesis 1 is arranged topically not sequentially, one is almost compelled to conclude

---

[37] Stated positively, how does Irons say both that the sun causes light and the sun does not cause light?

that days 2 and 5 are "two different perspectives on the same creative work." To the objection that the creation of the sea and expanse as well as the birds and sea creatures could not be the product of same creative act since they are so different, one needs only to observe how God created divergent objects in other singular creative acts. He created the sun, moon and stars, quite different objects, in one creative act (day 4). Indeed, he created the birds and sea creatures, two different kinds of creatures, in one creative act (day 5). It is not at all implausible that God created both the realm and rulers on the same day given these considerations.

A similar interpretation could be given to days 3 and 6. The imaginary framework exegete could, thus, come up with four creative acts during the creation week rather than eight.[38] But this leads to a problem. Given the principle of ordinary providence and given the nature of the objects created on this new understanding of the creative events, it will hardly do to maintain that these were created at different times. For God to create the luminaries at one time, the sea, expanse, birds and fishes at another, and the land, vegetation, animals and man at yet another is not, *ex hypothesis*, possible. Birds, for example, would either be created before land (where would they nest? what would they eat?) or after. But if land was created before birds then so were the land animals (and man!). But how could the land animals survive without the expanse (atmosphere)? The four distinct creative events makes nonsense out of the principle of ordinary providence. The imaginary exegete is forced to conclude that these fiats are really different perspectives on the same creative work. But what creative work is that? The answer is obvious. The creative work described in Genesis 1:1. Seven of the eight creative acts mentioned in the six days of creation thus may be understood as an expansion on the creation of the heavens and earth.[39]

One may object that if this were so, why does Genesis 1 record eight separate creative acts? And further, why does the author spend so much

---

[38] The creation of man would be understood to be a separate fiat on the basis of Genesis 2:7.

[39] Most Framework Hypothesis advocates will no doubt reject this interpretation. But notice that this is not only a plausible gloss of the text, given their other views, but it does not contradict other revelation. According the Majority Report, therefore, the Presbytery would have to accept framework candidates who did hold to this interpretation.

space describing how the world as we know it came about? One plausible answer (given the Framework Hypothesis) is that the creative acts of the creation week are a poetic way of expressing God's bringing the world to its present state in order for man to fill and dominate it. The separate creative acts, like the separate days, are not to be understood literally. One could then understand Genesis 1 to teach that God created all things out of nothing, but the product of his creation, which is initially described as null and void, was endowed with powers to differentiate and organize. The universe created at the beginning would thus inorganically as well as organically evolve until it reached its telos – an inhabitable environment for man, the image of God, who was created to exercise dominion over it.

The eight creative acts, thus, stand or fall together. If two are really just one described from different perspectives, the exegetical equivalent of Pandora's box is opened on Genesis 1.

Orthodox advocates of the framework interpretation would, of course, repudiate such an interpretation. Kline, for example, asserts that raising questions of ordinary providence during the creation week is "not to raise the question of whether Genesis 1 leaves the door open for some sort of evolutionary reconstruction." Indeed, Kline is adamant in denying that the ordered world is the product of such an evolutionary process: "... it is assumed here that Genesis 1 contradicts the idea that an undifferentiated world-stuff evolved into the present variegated universe by dint of intrinsic potentialities whether divinely 'triggered' or otherwise" (Kline, "Rain," 146). Kline's orthodoxy is appreciated. But an assumption is not proof. The question is not whether a framework advocate is orthodox on this point, but whether the Framework Hypothesis exegetically allows one to depart from orthodoxy. The above interpretation is a plausible gloss of Genesis 1, given the Framework advocates' other views. Indeed, one Framework Hypothesis exponent has come to just such a conclusion.

> But the *method* by which God achieved all this is not given. Was it by the separate instantaneous creation of each and every creature? Or was it by some process which , in the case of living things, began with some simple organism and arrived finally under the hand of God at the completed product, that is by some evolutionary process? In my view, the narrative in Genesis 1 yields no information about the divine method, only that, whatever the method, it was divine, so that any concept of a purely naturalistic evolution without God is ruled out. But there are alternatives to the two extreme positions of fiat creationism and naturalistic evolution,

and men of deep Christian conviction can be found who hold such intermediate positions as *theistic evolution* or *progressive creationism*. (Thompson 20).[40]

According the Majority Report, since such a view does not appear to contradict other revelation, it is consistent with the Confession's hermeneutic. And because it does not undeniably contradict Scripture, the Presbytery would have to accept framework candidates who held to this interpretation.

---

[40] A similar position can be adduced from Framework Hypothesis advocate, Ronald Youngblood. He concludes that only three things are taught in Genesis 1: (1) "God created the universe at the beginning of time;" (2) "God brought into being al the denizens of the universe;" (3) Creation is unfolded in a beautiful and orderly pattern... There is an unmistakable progression from simple to complex, from lower forms to higher..." Notice that Youngblood does not include *how* God created. Thus, progressive creationism is completely consistent with his position. See his "Moses and the King of Siam," *Journal of the Evangelical Theological Society* 16.4 (Fall 1973) 215-222.

PART III
CONFESSIONAL STUDIES

Chapter 5

THE RE-INTERPRETATION OF THE CONFESSION

Kenneth L. Gentry, Jr.

Introduction

Framework advocate Lee Irons wrote a response to David Hall's important 1998 speech to the Presbyterian Church in America General Assembly. In that speech Hall dealt with the meaning of the Westminster Standards' statement that creation occurred "in the space of six days." In his response titled "In the Space of Six Days: What Did the Divines Mean?"[1] Irons mounted an energetic critique of Hall's historical research into the original meaning of the Confession of Faith's statement.

Irons' assault was vigorous and unrelenting. But in the final analysis it serves to unmask the quiet desperation of the Framework Hypothesis and illustrate its ultimate Confessional failure. In our opinion, Irons' argument provides a clear example of the dangerous hermeneutical engine driving the Framework Hypothesis. As I shall show in this brief response, Irons' paper suffers from dialectical tension, conceptual confusion, and methodological absurdity. This is fortunate, however, in that had he sustained a successful argument he would have undermined the whole purpose of creeds themselves by evacuating the meaning of creedal assertions.

Basically, Irons attempted two bold and important ventures in his paper: (1) He strove to demonstrate the Confession's statement that God created the world "in the space of six days" is ambiguous. The Confession, he argued, merely parrots Scriptural language, thereby leaving the

---

[1] Presented on October 3, 1998, to the "Special Committee to Evaluate the Framework Hypothesis," Presbytery of Southern California of the Orthodox Presbyterian Church. Please note that the contents of this chapter were written in response to an internal report of the Committee, which was authored by Majority Committee member Lee Irons. Rev. Irons later withdrew his report and no longer argues that the divines left the Confession *intentionally ambiguous* regarding the nature of the days of creation. The reader should be aware, then, that Irons no longer holds the position appearing in his original report which I critique below. Nevertheless, I have chosen to include this critique in our book in that some Framework Hypothesis advocates still hold the "intentional ambiguity" argument. Hence, the potential value of the included material despite a change in historical circumstances.

interpretation of the "six days" of Creation to the individual subscriber. (2) He further argued that historical exegesis of the Confession proves that this ambiguity is intentional. By this maneuver he attempted to open the door to the Framework Hypothesis, while undercutting the traditional argument for six day creation.

As I shall show, Irons failed of both of his primary goals in his paper. In an effort to conserve space I will proceed through his paper in a seriatim fashion. But before I actually begin my response we must note the nature of the debate between the Framework Hypothesis and the Traditional Interpretation.

The section of the Westminster Confession of Faith in dispute is found in chapter 4, paragraph 1:

> It pleased God the Father, Son, and Holy Ghost, for the manifestation of the glory of His eternal power, wisdom, and goodness, in the beginning, to create, or make of nothing, the world, and all things therein whether visible or invisible, in the space of six days; and all very good.

Here the Confession of Faith presents Presbyterian Framework theorists with an immediate and embarrassing problem. The almost universal and historical consensus recognizes the Confession's statement "in the space of six days" as defining the time-frame of the original creative acts of God. The average English reader doubtlessly recognizes these words as setting temporal limits upon the original creative work of God. And herein is exposed the dangerous implications of the Framework Hypothesis: Not only does the Framework view discount the temporal delimiters structuring the Genesis 1 record itself ("evening/morning," solar function, ordinal prefixes, serial enumeration[2]), but it sets about refashioning the very simple and obvious language of our Confession.

The Framework Hypothesis would earn more respect among its opponents were its proponents to admit that the language of the Confession means what it actually says and then simply declare an exception at that point. But when we witness the attempt at re-interpreting the clear language before us, deep and serious concerns boil up. Where will this methodology

---

[2] See: Kenneth L. Gentry, Jr., "Reformed Theology and Six Day Creationism," *Christianity & Society* 5:4 (October, 1995): 25-29. Gerhard F. Hasel, "The 'Days' of Creation in Genesis 1: Literal 'Days' Or Figurative 'Periods/Epochs' of Time?", *Origins*, 21:1 (1994): 5-38. Berkhof, 154-55. Dabney, 254-56.

lead? What elements within the Confession are safe from the re-interpretive hermeneutic? And for how long are they safe once this interpretive approach is unleashed?

The Problem of Historical Exegesis

Irons opened his actual response to Hall's research in the writings of the Westminster divines with this rather surprising comment, a comment that exposes a fundamental flaw in Irons' effort:

> Hall does not seem to have asked himself a pertinent hermeneutical question. Can we assume that these views of these theologians is [*sic*] ultimately determinative for how we ought to interpret what the Confession itself actually says and does not say? In other words, just because many of the divines held a particular view of the days, does that necessarily imply that the Confession affirms a particular view of the days? (p.1)

Shortly thereafter he argued: "Studies of intellectual context are only of limited value with respect to the politics of confessional subscription" (p. 2).

When anyone compares WCF 4:1 with the Framework Hypothesis of Genesis 1, it becomes immediately obvious *why* Irons would want to question Hall's historical research: the views of the Confession's framers are incompatible with the Framework Hypothesis but perfectly fit the Traditionalist perspective. Irons' statement here at the very opening of his critique is remarkable in several respects:

(1) By this opening maneuver Irons effectively discounted the scholarly practice of historical exegesis. Yet in order to understand any historical document we *must* seek to discern the original intent of the author(s). Otherwise the whole interpretive enterprise becomes an exercise in eisegesis, leaving the document at the mercy of future fads and fashions. Hall's research analyzes the published writings of the framers (and others in their era) to discover their fuller thoughts on the matter before us. Their creedal formulation does not appear out of the blue, but within a particular intellectual context. Irons himself admits Hall "has assisted us in placing the Confession in its intellectual context" and that "Hall has provided many quotes useful for determining original intent" (Irons, p. 1).

(2) Such historical research as Hall provides us becomes absolutely indispensable in situations like that currently before us. Long after the framing of the Confession's article on creation, an entirely new view of the whole creation process has arisen. This new view directly contravenes the very clear and historically recognized language of the Confession. The Framework Hypothesis informs us that the days of Genesis do *not* instruct us on the passing of time as we now experience it. Rather Genesis speaks of something altogether different. In fact, rather than creation transpiring "in the space of six days," the Framework Hypothesis urges that "with respect to both the duration and sequence of events, the scientist is left free of biblical constraints in hypothesizing about cosmic origins."[3] Irons was correct in noting that "the Confession is what is binding, not the views of individual authors" (p. 2). The problem arises in that through Irons' argument, the Confession is being evacuated of its original intent. Such a maneuver demands that we research the wider body of literature produced by the divines to discover what they meant. The necessity of Hall's research, then, becomes all the more urgent due to the re-interpretive process necessary to make room for the Framework Hypothesis.

(3) This historical research becomes especially necessary in that the document in question is a creedal document. As the Latin etymology of "creed" instructs us and as creedalism has historically operated, a creed is a statement of *belief*, a pronouncement of commitment to a particular theological position. The whole purpose of a creed is to "lock-in" a particular theological viewpoint, to stand against the eroding tides of shifting fashion. Consequently, a creed must be understood in terms of its original intent or else it fails of its purpose, in that it does not secure a particular theological construct as a "platform for unity" (Irons, 2). The Traditional Interpretation vigorously and unashamedly proclaims that God created the universe "in the space of six days," just as does the Confession; the Framework Hypothesis argues that God most definitely did *not* create

---

[3] Meredith G. Kline, "Space and Time in the Genesis Cosmogony," *Perspectives on Science and Christian Faith*, 48 (1996):2.

in such a compacted time frame, due to God's use of natural providence in the creation process (based on insights derived from Gen. 2:5).[4]

(4) Furthermore, despite Irons' assertion, Hall's research does not "assume" the views of the framers of the Confession: it *documents* them. And it documents then in the light of the specific and clear statement within the Confession they framed. In various places in Irons' paper we find that certain of the views of the Westminster divines do *not* appear in creedal form in the Confession of Faith: the young earth, the date of the creation, the season of the creation. Yet in 4:1 we *do* discover their view on the *time-frame* of the creational activity of God.

(5) Ironically, Irons himself allowed historical exegesis to demonstrate that "the Westminster divines specifically rejected the Augustinian view. . . . There can be no doubt that 'in the space of six days,' both in Calvin and the Confession, was intended to rule out the instantaneous creation view" (p. 5). Though he complained of Hall's "selective" use of historical argument (see the next point), it seems that Irons himself was selective in his denouncing the use of historical exegesis.

(6) A little later in his paper Irons made a startling statement that as seriously misrepresents Hall's research as it does misconstrue the nature of the historical exegetical enterprise:

> Hall's appeal to the weight of church history is arbitrary. On the one hand, he wants us to avoid the hubris of the modern mindset which rejects the ancient in favor of the new, and which always assumes that newer is better. But on the other hand, he selectively decides which ecclesiastical

---

[4] For example, Kline writes: "Gen. 2:5 reflects an environmental situation that has obviously lasted for a while; it assumes a far more leisurely pace on the part of the Creator, for whom a thousand years are as one day." "Gen. 2:5, however, takes it for granted that providential operations were not of a supernatural kind, but that God ordered the sequence of creation acts so that the continuance and development of the earth and its creatures could proceed by natural means. This unargued assumption of Gen. 2:5 contradicts the re constructions of the creation days proposed by the more traditional views." "The more traditional interpretations of the creation account are guilty not only of creating a conflict between the Bible and science but, in effect, of pitting Scripture against Scripture." "All the vast universe whose origin is narrated on day four would then be younger (even billions of years younger) than the speck in space called earth. So much for the claimed harmony of the narrative sequence of Genesis with scientific cosmology." Meredith G. Kline, "Space and Time in the Genesis Cosmogony," *Perspectives on Science and Christian Faith*, 48:2-15 (March, 1996). See also: Charles Lee Irons, "The Framework Interpretation Explained and Defended" (by the author: February 4, 1998), 35-36.

traditions are allowed to count. The traditions of 19th century American Presbyterianism and Old Princeton are dismissed as being too recent. But by what authority does Hall determine the cut-off point of legitimate 'old' traditions?" (p. 4).

This remarkable error cannot be allowed to pass unnoticed. Note that:

(a) Hall's appeal to church history is not in the least "arbitrary." Hall is engaged in *historical exegesis* for the purpose of determining *original intent*. Consequently, he cites from the "intellectual context" (to use Irons' own phrase, p. 1) in which the Confession was framed. The *problem* before us is that *later* observations and re-interpretations of the Confession have evacuated the Confessional statement of its historical meaning. Perhaps diachronically mapping out the development of Confessional interpretations would prove an interesting study, but this is not the issue before us.

(b) Contrary to Irons' assertion Hall is not interested in the least with "old" v. "new," but with *original intent* v. *contemporary re-interpretation*. The two concerns (old/new v. original/contemporary) are not equatable in the least. At times in Irons' paper he seemed to understand this, but then he appeared to forget the matter when drawing conclusions.

Returning to the same paragraph on Irons' page 1 (regarding "the pertinent hermeneutical question"), Irons continued his assault upon historical exegesis of the Confession: "Just because many of the divines held a particular view of the days, does that necessarily imply that the Confession affirms a particular view of the days?" (p. 1). In response let me note the following:

(1) Irons admitted that "many of the divines" hold the natural day view of Genesis 1. He confessed that Hall "has located a large number of quotes from the 17th century Reformed theologians which indicate the possible presence of a consensus on several points relative to the days of creation" (p. 1). In point of fact, Hall not only provided us a large array of evidence in this direction in his original paper, but he has since added several new references from the divines: the body of evidence is growing.[5] How can we dismiss the divines' convictions on the Genesis creation account when interpreting their Confession? Especially when a proposed interpretation counters those convictions?

---

[5] Including references from William Gouge, William Twisse, Charles Herle, Daniel Cawdrey, Herbert Palmer, Adoniram Byfield, and John Arrowsmith.

(2) Irons did not offer even *one* countervailing assertion by a Westminster divine. There appears to be no dispute among the divines as to the nature of the creation days. The dispute is a modern cavil that has suspiciously arisen since the appearance of scientific evolutionism and its demand for enormous time-frames (not that Irons, Kline, or their associates are sympathetic to evolution).

(3) The extra-Confessional statements of the divines do not *imply* that the Confession "affirms a particular view of the days." Rather the Confession itself (as we shall see in a little more detail shortly) *affirms* God created "in the space of six days," thereby fitting perfectly with the framers' other writings.

The Failure of Irons' Analysis

Irons complained: "assuming that these men almost universally held to a young earth, logically we cannot conclude that the Confession itself affirms or requires the young earth position" (p. 2). In response I would note:

(1) Irons' choice of terms unfortunately tended to bias his readers against Hall's work: once again he speaks of "assuming" something. Hall does not *assume* the young earth perspective of the divines: he provides what Irons himself calls "a catalogue of quotes," that is, he *documents* their views.

(2) But theoretically the young earth viewpoint differs from the six day position in an important respect in our Confessional debate: the Confession *does* assert God created "in the space of six days." The Traditional view does not require that *the Confession* asserts a young earth; that position is conceptually distinct.

(3) Irons missed the point of Hall's citing young earth evidence from the divines. He did not cite the young earth statements in order to demand a young earth perspective for creedal subscription. Rather he was demonstrating from the intellectual context of the divines that their creedal statement "in the space of six days" cannot be extrapolated out into multiple billions of years, as allowed in the Framework Hypothesis and evolutionary theory. Whatever the age of the earth is, it did not come to that allegedly advanced age *during the creation week*, for the Confession directly informs us that that week only covered "the space of six days."

Irons attempted to undercut Hall's research by commenting on the debate over the season of the year in which the original creation week occurred, whether it was "in the spring or the fall" (p. 2). He noted that this issue was "not resolved" among Reformed theologians. Then he makes the self-destructive observation:

> Clearly, then, it was a question that could have been debated at the Westminster Assembly and the majority view could have been enshrined in the Confession itself. Yet we find no references to this question in the Confession. Is it not obvious that the Assembly did not consider this issue to be relevant to the Confession's purpose and scope? (p. 2)

This comment actually strengthens our argument against the Framework Hypothesis:

(1) As a matter of fact the divines *did* include a statement concerning the length of the creation week. Consequently, on Irons' own method this *is* "relevant to the Confession's purpose and scope." What is more, the fact of original creation transpiring "in the space of six days" is so important that it not only appears in the Confession of Faith but also in both the Larger and Shorter Catechisms:

> Larger Catechism Question 15: What is the work of creation? Answer: The work of creation is that wherein God did in the beginning, by the word of his power, make of nothing the world, and all things therein, for himself, within the space of six days, and all very good.

> Shorter Catechism Question 9: What is the work of creation? Answer: The work of creation is, God's making all things of nothing, by the word of his power, in the space of six days, and all very good.

(2) It exposed the serious danger inherent in Irons' Confessional exegetical methodology. If Irons argued that the absence of a clear statement from the Confession is *telling evidence* against its significance, then we cannot argue that God created the *entire universe*! The Confession says *nothing* about the creation of the universe when it states:

> It pleased God the Father, Son, and Holy Ghost, for the manifestation of the glory of His eternal power, wisdom, and goodness, in the beginning, to create, or make of nothing, the world, and all things therein whether visible or invisible, in the space of six days; and all very good.

> After God had made all other creatures, He created man, male and female, with reasonable and immortal souls, endued with knowledge, righteousness, and true holiness, after His own image; (WCF 4:1-2a)

Notice that the Confession only mentions the creation of "the world" and the creatures in it (cp. also LC 15). Elsewhere it only alludes to "the beginning of the *world*" (LC 116; SC 59).

Returning again to his bias against historical exegesis, we may note that Irons wrote: "Notice the fallacy of Hall's argument. 'The *context* of Westminster's original intent' as defined 'in their other writings' must interpret what the Confession itself actually says'" (p. 3). In response I would comment:

(1) Where is the *fallacy* in this? Is this not common, scholarly historical exegesis? Again Irons' complaint does not reflect the actual situation in Hall's work.

(2) Did not Irons himself (pp. 1, 5) assert that the language "in the space of six days" is the divines' response to Augustine's conception? And how did he know that? *On the basis of historical exegesis of the divines other writings!* "Hall correctly argues that the Westminster divines specifically rejected the Augustinian view in its 'in the space of six days' language" (p. 5).

(3) Furthermore, where does the Confession itself allow any other view than that creation transpired "in the space of six days"? The Confession and Catechisms consistently maintain that view. Indeed, the Standards assert that the seventh day sabbath prevailed "from the beginning of the world to the resurrection of Christ" (WCF 21:7; LC 116; SC 59). Obviously the sabbath is established *after* the creation process, yet it is deemed extant "from the beginning of the world." Furthermore, in that man himself is a part of the original creation process "in the beginning," how can the Framework Hypothesis allow a multi-billion year old earth (see footnote 4 above) which places man *late* in the scheme of things *far* from "the beginning"? Do the Standards not demand the appearance of man upon the earth "from the beginning" (WCF 8:6; as does Scripture, Matt. 19:4; Mark 10:6)?

Evidence of the strain placed upon Irons' presentation appears in various overstatements and misconceptions, such as the one we come upon at this point in his paper: Irons erroneously argues that "the divines would have known only two possibilities: either an eternal world, or a world about 6,000 years old." In fact, "a very old universe" was "not within the realm of intellectual possibility for them" (p. 3). This is obviously overstated in that:

(1) Turretin (a Reformed writer cited by Irons and living in the time of the divines) muses theoretically: "Thus the duration of the world might have been of many more ages than it actually is; so that from the beginning of the world to the present time, there might have flowed by not only five or six million years, but seven or nine. And yet you could not rightly infer from this that therefore the world might have been created from eternity because the consequence does not hold good from a longer, finite and bounded duration . . . to an eternal and infinite duration."[6] Obviously it was "intellectually" possible for them to contemplate a very old world beyond 6,000 years old.

(2) Irons himself admitted in the paragraph preceding the one containing his statement: Hall "shows that prior to the 19th century, it is *rare* to find an orthodox theologian arguing for an old earth" (p. 3). If it is "rare" it is not beyond the realm of possibility for it was in fact considered, even if not frequently.

(3) In Hall's paper, which had been read by Irons, Hall cites Ussher's *Sum and Substance of Christian Religion* wherein Ussher affirmed a young earth and argued that one of the reasons for this was "to convince all heathen, that either thought that the world was without beginning, or that it began millions of years before it did" that they are mistaken (Hall, p. 9).

As an aside, but illustrating Irons' inadvertent tendency to overstate and misconstrue evidence, Irons misrepresents Turretin when he brought him into the discussion *in the way* in which he does: "When Turretin discusses the question 'Was the world from eternity, or at least could it have been?', he appeals to the 'six thousand years' of sacred history recorded in Scripture as evidence for the world's non-eternity" (p. 3). Irons' unwary reader would doubtless get the impression that this is either Turretin's only argument or his major one. Yet Turretin *begins* his argument two pages prior to this offending statement with numerous biblical references to the fact of creation by God — irrespective of the *date* of the earth's origin. In other words, the *date of the earth's creation* is not a first order or necessary argument.

---

[6] Francis Turretin, *Institutes of Elenctic Theology*, trans. by George Musgrave Giger, edited by James T. Dennison, Jr. (Phillipsburg, N. J.: P & R Publishing, rep. 1992), 441.

The Awkwardness of the Intentional Obscurity Argument

Having misconstrued the nature of the enterprise before us, Irons finally came to "the meaning of 'in the space of six days'" (p. 4). His presentation was then in a full-scale decline into self-contradiction.

Of Hall's documentation showing the divines believed in a literal six day creation, Irons argued "Hall's evidence points in the opposite direction" (p. 4). After citing five illustrations from the theologians of the 17th century showing statements about "a natural day" and "twenty foure howres," Irons made the incredible and excited leap of logic: "But such qualifying expressions were not included in the Confession! The phrases 'natural day' and 'consisting of 24 hours' are nowhere to be found either in the Confession or the Catechisms. . . . Does not this suggest an original intent on their part to leave the Confession ambiguous by simply quoting the language of Scripture?" (p. 4). But note the following rejoinders:

(1) Irons overlooked the important fact that the Confession of Faith is a *creed*, not a *systematic theology*. It is a *statement*, not an *exposition*. It *summarizes* doctrinal truth; it does not *expand* upon it.

(2) The evidence Hall provides leads *precisely* and *inexorably* to Hall's conclusion. And this despite Irons' vain attempt to breathe life into Alexander Mitchell's long discounted argument otherwise. In that creeds are *summations* of doctrine and in that all the evidence presented by Hall[7] that the Westminster divines and 17th century theologians held to twenty-four hour days, we can easily understand how they could employ the shorthand phrase "in the space of six days" to represent their view. Were there contrary views floating among Reformed scholars and being debated in their day, perhaps they would have provided a fuller statement — although as I will show and as common sense dictates, their phrase admirably accomplishes its purpose in relating their view of a literal six day creation.

(3) In the examples cited in his attempt to prop up his weak, counter-intuitive, contra-historical argument, Irons reminded us of the allegedly damaging nature of the Reformed commitment to six day creation in the

---

[7] Note that Hall profusely documents the 24-hour convictions of numerous divines, that Irons' basically admits this as the prevailing view, and that Irons provides no countervailing evidence to the contrary.

17th century. Note *how* his select quotations provided clues as to *why* it was not necessary to expand upon the phrase: Richardson's quote observes that the term "day" in his view *"must have* comprehended twenty four hours." White notes quite simply that "it *signifies* a natural day." Dort's observation is that this is "the *meaning* of these words." If the word in question "must" mean such, if it "signifies" that, if it is its "meaning," *why would the divines have to belabor the obvious*?

(4) Again, it appears to Traditional advocates that the "problem" with the phrase "in the space of six days" arises *not* from any ambiguity in the Confession, nor from the original convictions of the divines. But rather the "problem" arises *at least in part* from recent concerns (since the late 1800s) that Christians must recognize the enormous time frames demanded by natural revelation brought to us in modern geology.[8] In other words, a confessional *problem* seems to have been manufactured because of our contemporary debate with the current convictions of geological scientists. The Confession's *language* is not the problem, but rather the Confession's *theology*. Irons' strained hermeneutical approach to the Confession, misconstruction of the historical evidence, and confusion of the nature of the debate is at least partly related to the problem of the "assured" conclusions (Irons' calls it "all the evidence," pp. 3-4) of the geological timetable.

Irons complained against the Traditional construction of the Confession: "Does not this suggest an original intent in their part to leave the Confession ambiguous by simply quoting the language of Scripture?" (p. 4). But note:

(1) Actually the language "in the space of six days" is quite easily understandable, and necessarily presents a literalistic construction of the record in Genesis 1. Ask anyone on the street what the statement "in the space of six days" signifies.

---

[8] "The conclusion is that as far as the time frame is concerned, with respect to both the duration and sequence of events, the scientist is left free of biblical constraints in hypothesizing about cosmic origins." "The more traditional interpretations of the creation account are guilty . . . of creating a conflict between the Bible and science." "In this article I have advocated an interpretation of biblical cosmogony according to which Scripture is open to the current scientific view of a very old universe and, in that respect, does not discountenance the theory of the evolutionary origin of man" (fn 47). Kline, "Space and Time" 15. I should note that Kline does *not* personally adopt "the evolutionary origin of man" but holds to "Adam as an historical individual" (fn 47).

(2) Furthermore, the Confession does *not* engage in "simply quoting the language of Scripture" (p. 4) — as if *that* were evidence *against* its obvious meaning! Actually the exact phrase is not found in Scripture, for the divines state it in two different, though similar ways: "in the space of six days" (WCF 4:1) and "within the space of six days" (LC 15). The phrase "in the space of" or "within the space of" clearly indicates the notion of a temporal time frame.

(3) In fact, the phrase "in the space of" has a relevant history. As Irons admits, it derives from John Calvin's commentary on Genesis 2:5, where we read:

> It is too violent a cavil to contend that Moses distributes the work which God perfected at once into six days, for the mere purpose of conveying instruction. Let us rather conclude that God himself took the space of six days, for the purpose of accommodating his works [*not* his *revelation* of his works — KLG] to the capacity of men. . . He distributed the creation of the world [*not* the *revelation* of it — KLG] into successive portions.

Later at Genesis 2:3 Calvin reminds his reader: "I have said above, that six days were employed in the formation of the world."

Calvin's statement is the historical backdrop of the language of the Confession. Even Irons confessed: "It is well-known that the phrase 'in the space of' was first used by Calvin in order to distance himself from Augustine's view . . . . Hall states this phrase 'was adopted by the Westminster Assembly.' And I have no reason to question Hall's assertion" (p. 5).

Indeed, in *Augustine's* writing on the subject — the writings to which Hall and Irons suggest the divines were responding — he himself mentions "in the space of" as a temporal designation that he is opposing. And Irons knows this, for it appears in Hall's research where he comments: "In *The Literal Meaning of Genesis*, Augustine the alleged adherent of the Framework Hypothesis commented: 'Hence it seems that this work of God was done in the space of a day.'"

Hall continues:

> Perhaps most definitive of the view of the Divines is John White (an "Assessor" for the Assembly) who wrote a lengthy *Commentary on the First Three Chapters of Genesis* (London, 1656). He, too, followed Ussher's understanding of days and chronology (p. 3), and assuredly did not envision a long period of a geologic age as a doctrinal possibility.

Most clearly, this Westminster Divine set forth his opinion, that is uncontradicted by the other divines: "Here, where it [day, *yom*] is distinguished from the Night, it is taken for a Civil day, that is, that part of 24 houres which is Light; but in the latter end of the verse, it signifies a Natural day, consisting of 24 houres, and includes the night too." (p. 32) Moreover, "By the Evening, we must here understand the whole night, or space between the shutting in of the light, and the dawning of the next day. . . . In the same manner runs the computation of Times, among the Hebrews to this day." (32) White's use of the term "space" and his reference to "God is here represented to us, in the Creation of the world, proceeding by leisure, and taking the time of Six dayes to perform that . . ." indicates that the Westminster divines had a definite meaning for the phrase "in the space of" that was not merely a summary for large, undefined periods of time.

(4) In the final analysis we must remember that the Framework Hypothesis does not allow the phrase "in the space of six days" to speak of a passage of time anyway. According to Irons, the six day structure of Genesis 1 is a "literary device intentionally crafted by the author" that cannot be temporally constrained, so that "the days are not literal days."[9] Again the Confession says the creation transpired "in the space of six days"; the Framework Hypothesis says it did *not*. What could be more diametrically opposed?

(5) On another, tangentially-related question Irons argued: "It is entirely conceivable that the Westminster divines intentionally left the question of the age of the earth undecided in the Confession" (p. 1). If that is their practice and their intent in certain areas, why then did they bother including in the Confession the misleading comment "in the space of six days"? Had they omitted the offending phrase their purpose would have been better served, rather than by inserting it as an "intentionally . . . ambiguous" assertion in a document they declare is their "confession of faith." Who wants an "ambiguous" confession of faith? The tenuous nature of Irons' argument is exposed by the fact that he offers no evidence whatsoever: he cites no debate over the phrase, he points to no countervailing opinions among the divines — he simply asserts it as his confession of faith! As Irons shows us, the divines were quite capable of leaving interesting,

---

[9] Irons, "The Framework Interpretation Explained and Defended," 27.

debated subjects out of their Confession (e.g., the age of the earth, the season of its creation).

Conclusion

The matter before us is extremely important due to the temper of our times. The secular hegemony of naturalistic evolutionism has presented the Church a tremendous worldview challenge. The implications of evolution (and its step-child modern geology) are so wide-ranging and all-penetrating that its inherent relativism have led to dangerous principles of linguistic interpretation. These have even resulted ultimately in a deconstructionist hermeneutic that destroys all meaning in any given text.

The traditional interpretation of the Genesis record stands contrary to evolutionism. Our Confession of Faith as evangelical, conservative Presbyterians also stands against evolutionary theory — not only in asserting the divine origin of the universe and the special creation of man (which Framework Interpreters join with us in affirming — as over against evolutionary theory), but also in setting forth the time-frame within which God's creative fiats transpired.

Those committed to the traditional, historical exegesis of Genesis 1 are concerned that our Confession is being handled in a disingenuous way when attempts are made to re-interpret its objective, unambiguous statements. If in the final analysis six day creation is erroneous, we are convinced that we would have more integrity as a church before the world if we simply revised our Confession by deleting the offending phrase, rather than altering its clear and forthright meaning.

149

Chapter 6
ADDITIONAL ATTEMPTS AROUND THE CONFESSION
Michael R. Butler

In this Chapter I will provide additional scrutiny of the Framework Hypothesis in terms of the Westminster Standards beyond that which Gentry provides in the preceding chapter. These matters are important issues for Presbyterians reckoning with the Framework Hypothesis. And they are insightful even for those not ordained in Presbyterianism in that the insights provide further demonstration of the desperation of the Framework Hypothesis proponents who press the issue in Presbyterian circles.

The *Animus Imponentis*

Some have argued that Presbyterian confessional subscription should not be a barrier to accepting the Framework Hypothesis due to the *animus imponentis*, i. e., the intention of the imposing body. The *animus imponentis* speaks of a confessional vow as a commitment to the confession *as understood by the church imposing the vow*. While the right of a church to interpPret her confession of faith is certainly something that has been recognized in historic Presbyterianism, the following are some strictures upon this practice:

1) The original intention of a confessional document must be the normal and assumed meaning of the document when it is adopted by the church.

2) Recognizing, however, that confessions are human documents and that the Spirit speaking in the Scriptures is alone the final authority, there may be occasions when the original intention of a confession must be altered or clarified in order to more fully comply with the teaching of Scripture.

3) The *only* legitimate reason for altering or clarifying the original intention of a confession is to make the confession more fully accord with Scripture.

4) Consequently, it is an abuse of the principle of the *animus imponentis* to reinterpret a confession *solely* on the basis of making the

interpretation broad enough to accommodate differences of opinions among the church's officers.

5) The alteration or clarifying of the meaning of a confessional document may legitimately come about in only two ways: (a) the church may revise the wording of her confession; (b) the church may keep the original wording of her confession but reinterpret its meaning.

6) If the church reinterprets her confession without revising its wording, it must be done consciously and in full knowledge by the entire church.

7) The church may only legitimately reinterpret the original intention of a confession if the reinterpretation is within the possible range of meaning of the particular portion of the confession in question.

8) The reinterpretation of the church's confession is normally and preferably done by an official declaration of the church.

9) In the *abnormal* case of the church reinterpreting her confession without an official declaration, the reinterpretation must still be done by consciously and in full knowledge of the entire body.

10) Consequently, it is illegitimate for a church to, in practice, "reinterpret" her confession by means of theological laxity on the part of her officers or by historical accident.

Time and space constraints do not permit me to give a defense of each of these propositions. Hopefully, their legitimacy is apparent.

Applying these strictures to the Framework Hypothesis, it becomes clear that it fails on three counts. First, it fails in regards to (3). Given that the *only* legitimate reason for altering or clarifying the original intention of a confession is to make the confession more fully accord with Scripture, if the original intention of the Westminster Confession was to teach a literal 24-hour creation, as it clearly was, and if, as we have argued elsewhere in this Report, the Framework Hypothesis is not in accord with Scripture, then the original intention of the Westminster Confession must not be altered.

Second, the Framework Hypothesis fails in regards to (6), (8) and (9). No Presbyterian church has formally declared the meaning of "in the space of six days" to be anything other than its original intention (8). Moreover, a reinterpretation of the meaning of these words has never been accomplished consciously and in full knowledge of the entire body (9). Therefore, because a reinterpretation of the meaning of "in the space of six days" has not been accomplished, the framework interpretation is not in accord with the teaching of the Confession.

Three, the Framework Hypothesis fails in regards to (7). It is not within the possible range of meaning of the phrase, "in the space of six days," to be reinterpreted in such a way as to make it accord with the Framework Hypothesis. This phrase expresses that God's acts of creation were accomplished within a definite duration and by a definite sequence. The original intention of the document was to declare that God created all things in the duration of six sequential, 24-hour days. However, it is within the possible range of meaning of this phrase to reinterpret it to mean that God created in the space or duration of six sequential ages.[1] It may even be within the possible range of meaning to reinterpret it to mean "in the space or duration of six non-sequential ages." But since the phrase, 'in the space of six days,' marks off a definite span of time, it is not within the possible range of meaning to reinterpret this phrase in such a way that it has no reference to any duration whatsoever. Since, therefore, the Framework Hypothesis clearly maintains that the Bible does not teach anything about the duration of God's acts of creation, it is not within the possible range of this phrase's meaning.[2]

Confessional Contradiction

In addition to properly resolving the *animus imponentis* question, we must recognize the serious question of debilitating *contradiction* in a confessional system. Additional concerns arise for those allowing the Framework Hypothesis to enter into a confessional environment by means of either re-interpreting the Confession or the *animus imponentis*. Consider the following complications.

---

[1] In saying this, it should not be inferred that I believe this is a legitimate understanding of the wording of the Confession.

[2] Framework advocates will object: "but we do believe that God created in six solar days, we just do not take those days literally." But if not literally, in what sense do they take 'days'? In reading the literature of the recognized advocates of the framework interpretation it is clear what they mean – either "upper-register" days or "anthropomorphic" days. But notice, however, that the English word, 'day,' never has, by itself, the meaning of "upper-register day" or "anthropomorphic day." (Consult the *Oxford English Dictionary* for proof.) In order for 'day' to mean either of these two things, an modifier is necessary. Thus in order for the framework interpretation to comport with the Confession a revision is called for.

It Contradicts the Confessional Teaching.

(1) The Framework Hypothesis explicitly denies the teaching of the Confession and both Catechisms regarding the sequence and duration of God's creative activity.

> It pleased God the Father, Son, and Holy Ghost, for the manifestation of the glory of His eternal power, wisdom, and goodness, in the beginning, to create, or make of nothing, the world, and all things therein whether visible or invisible, *in the space of six days*; and all very good. (WCF IV. 1)

> The work of creation is that wherein God did in the beginning, by the word of his power, made of nothing the world, and all things therein, for himself, within the space of six days, and all very good. (LC 15)

> The work of creation is, God's making all things of nothing, by the word of his power, in the space of six days, and all very good. (SC Q. 9)

(2) The Framework Hypothesis explicitly contradicts the teaching of our Standards regarding its declaration that the Sabbath ordinance was in effect from the beginning of world – i.e. when God created the world in the space of six days.

> As it is the law of nature, that, in general, a due proportion of time be set apart for the worship of God; so, in His Word, by a positive, moral, and perpetual commandment binding all men in all ages, He has particularly appointed one day in seven, for a Sabbath, to be kept holy unto him: which, *from the beginning of the world* to the resurrection of Christ, was the last day of the week: and, from the resurrection of Christ, was changed into the first day of the week, which, in Scripture, is called the Lord's Day, and is to be continued to the end of the world, as the Christian Sabbath. (WCF XXI. 7)

> The fourth commandment requireth of all men the sanctifying or keeping holy to God such set times as he hath appointed in his word, expressly one whole day in seven; which was the seventh *from the beginning of the world* to the resurrection of Christ, and the first day of the week ever since, and so to continue to the end of the world; which is the Christian Sabbath, and in the New Testament called "The Lord's day." (LC 116)

> *From the beginning of the world* to the resurrection of Christ, God appointed the seventh day of the week to be the weekly Sabbath; and the first day of the week ever since, to continue to the end of the world, which is the Christian sabbath. (SC 59)

The Framework Hypothesis explicitly contradicts the teaching of our Standards regarding its declaration that the Sabbath ordinance is grounded in the example of God's creative work.

> The reasons annexed to the fourth commandment, the more to enforce it, are taken from the equity of it, God allowing us six days of seven for our own affairs, and reserving but one for himself, in these words, "Six days shalt thou labor, and do all thy work:" from God's challenging a special propriety in that day, "The seventh day is the sabbath of the Lord they God:" *from the example of God, who "in six days made heaven and earth, the sea, and all that in them is, and rested the seventh day:"* and from that blessing which God put upon that day, not only in sanctifying it to be a day for his service, but in ordaining it to be a means of blessing to us in our sanctifying it; "Wherefore the Lord blessed the sabbath-day and hallowed it." (LC 120)

> The reasons annexed to the fourth commandment are, God's allowing us six days of the week for our own employments, his challenging a special propriety in the seventh, *his example*, and his blessing the sabbath-day. (SC 62)

It Contradicts an Essential Component of the Confession

Our Standards deem the doctrine of the duration and sequence of God's work of creation that they used the phrase "in the space of six days" or "within the space of six days" every time the doctrine of creation is defined.

It is apparent that the order and structure of the Confession of Faith are such that foundational issues of major consequence are placed first. The Confession of Faith is not a haphazard collection of doctrinal maxims, neither is it a systematic theological approach to doctrine. Instead it has an essential overall harmony that proceeds along a clear line of development: it first lays down foundational matters, then builds upon those in a logical and coherent fashion. As Philip Schaff notes: "The Confession consists of thirty-three chapters, which cover, in natural order, all the leading articles of the Christian faith from the creation to the final judgment."[3]

William Hetherington's classic work on the Confession elaborates a little more fully:

---

[3] Schaff, *The Creeds of Christendom* (Grand Rapids: Baker, rep. 1990), 1:766.

The first thing which must strike any thoughtful reader, after having carefully and studiously perused the Westminster Assembly's Confession of Faith, is the remarkable comprehensiveness and accuracy of its character, viewed as a systematic exhibition of divine truth, or what is termed a system of theology. In this respect it may be regarded as almost perfect, both in its arrangement and in its completeness. Even a single glance over its table of contents will show with what exquisite skill its arrangement proceeds, from the statement of first principles to the regular development and final consummation of the whole scheme of revealed truth.... Thus viewed, the Confession of Faith might be so connected with one aspect of Church history as to furnish, if not a text-book according to chronological arrangement, in studying the rise and refutation of heresies, yet a valuable arrangement of their relative importance, doctrinally considered....

A few remarks may be made with regard to the plan according to which the Confession is constructed. A Confession of Faith is simply a declaration of belief in religious truths, not scientifically discovered by man, but divinely revealed to man. While, therefore, there may fairly be a question whether a course of Systematic Theology should begin with disquisitions relative to the being and character of God, as revealed, or with an inquiry what Natural Theology can teach, proceeding thence to the doctrines of Revelation, there can be no question that a Confession of Faith in revealed religion ought to begin with that revelation itself. This is the plan adopted by the Westminster Confession. It begins with a chapter on the Holy Scriptures; then follow four chapters on the nature, decrees, and works of God in creation and providence: and these five chapters form a distinct division, systematically viewed, of the Confession."[4]

In other words, foundational to the "system of doctrine" contained in the Confession and "sincerely received and adopted" by elders in the Orthodox Presbyterian Church are the first five chapters of the Confession. Note the foundational logic of the Confession:

Chapter 1 secures for us the infallible means whereby we know God, His will, and ways, i.e., through Scripture. May we deny God speaks infallibly and inerrantly in Scripture? May we deny any of the sixty-six books of Scripture? This chapter establishes for us our ultimate authority for

---

[4] William M. Hetherington, *History of the Westminster Assembly of Divines* (Edmonton, AB: Still Waters Revival, 1887, rep. 1991), 350, 351, 357.

framing our system of doctrine: the Word of God contained in the Old and New Testaments. All else fails in our doctrinal system if this chapter is not true

Chapter 2 moves quite necessarily to the nature and being of the God whom we worship and serve. Which elements of our statement regarding the being of Almighty God may we remove? He is our very reason for existence. Indisputably chapter 2 must also be foundational to the whole system of doctrine contained in the Confession.

Chapter 3 flows quite logically into a consideration of the decrees of God, which explain, uphold, and direct the entire universe. The God we worship and serve is a sovereign Who planned all things by His eternal decree. This sets Christianity against all forms of unbelief and establishes our reason for serving the Lord God: He is absolutely sovereign. It explains also the rationality, significance, and value of the universe as rooted in the eternal plan of God.

Chapters 4 and 5 turn to consider the very creation of the entire universe and all of its elements and the actual outworking of the decree of God in providence. This is the arena in which man will live in the service of God: a God-created, God-governed universe. Nothing other than God Himself accounts for the existence and control of all reality. The stage is set for considering the following doctrinal formulations of our faith and practice in the world God created and governs. A denial of the Confessional position on creation is a denial of a foundational principle of the Confession and our "system of doctrine."

(3) The statement, "in the space of six days," moreover, is seen to be tied into the "system" of doctrine not only because of its ubiquity, its being an essential aspect of the doctrine of creation, and its being part of the foundational portion of the Confession, but also in its connection with the Sabbath ordinance. Our Standards tie the doctrines of creation and the Sabbath together. It is thus not an insignificant phrase that can be harmlessly laid aside. It is an essential component of the Confession's system of doctrine.

(4) The statement, "in the space of six days," is the only part of our Standards that confessionally keeps the teaching of progressive creationism and theistic evolution out of the Orthodox Presbyterian Church. Thus to either re-interpret the phrase or allow an exception to it effectively declares

that our church is silent as to God's mode of creation and opens the doors to these grave errors.

It Contradicts a Distinctive Teaching of the Standards.

Of all the Reformed symbols, only the Westminster Confession and Catechisms lay emphasis on the Sabbath ordinance. By denying our church's Standards regarding the grounding of this ordinance in God's creative activity, the Framework Hypothesis undermines the ordinance itself and with it a distinctive aspect of historic Presbyterianism.

The Confession asserts:

> All things in Scripture are not alike plain in themselves, nor alike clear unto all: yet those things which are necessary to be known, believed, and observed for salvation are so clearly propounded, and opened in some place of Scripture or other, that not only the learned, but the unlearned, in a due use of the ordinary means, may attain unto a sufficient understanding of them. (WCF 1: 7)

The Framework Hypothesis implies that Genesis 1 and 2, the two opening chapters of the first book of the Bible that sets the stage for all of redemptive history, that contains the seat of doctrine (*sedes doctrinae*) for Scripture's teaching on fundamentally important issue of creation, and that provides the very basis of the human work cycle and Sabbath day rest, has been fundamentally misunderstood by the church for almost 2000 years.

Over against the traditional, historic understanding of Genesis 1 and 2 by Christ's Church, the Framework Hypothesis introduces a completely novel interpretation of the text based upon convoluted reasoning and a highly sophisticated use of historical, semantic, literary and redemptive-historical analysis. This novel interpretation not only denies that the text teaches what appears to be the obvious duration and sequence of God's creative acts, but implies animal death before the fall and that the results of man's sin were almost exclusively spiritual in nature (the creation was not greatly affected by the curse), while at the same time it leaves open the possibility of progressive creationism and theistic evolution.

Not only is the reasoning of these two leading framework advocates convoluted and the implications of their view troublesome, but the conclusions they draw from these texts border on the fantastic. Kline, for example, says he demonstrates:

how two-register cosmology informs and shapes the treatment of both the space and time dimensions in the Genesis prologue. It is found that a metaphorical relationship exists between the two levels; the heavenly level (upper register) is described in figures drawn from the earthly level (lower register). As for the seven-day scheme, it belongs to the upper register and is, therefore, to be understood figuratively, not literally. (Kline, "Space and Time," 2)

Additionally, Futato, in an article he views as complementary to Kline's two-register cosmology view of Genesis 1, finds other novelties in the text: "These structural considerations lead to new insights into the polemical theology of Genesis 1-2. Genesis 1-2 serves, among other purposes, as a polemic against Canaanite Baalism." (Futato, 1-2) Thus, in Genesis 1 and 2 we find at least two novel teachings. These chapters teach a "two-register cosmology" while at the same time strongly warn against the worship of Baal. In other words, Genesis 1 and 2 takes us to the very throne room of God with all its angelic hosts and majestic splendor while at the same time warns against worshiping a provincial pagan deity. But what the text does not teach is that God created the world in six days.

If this is correct, the church has not understand these two basic features of Genesis 1 and 2 until 1996 and 1998 respectively. We should wonder why God expressed himself the way he did if this is indeed what he meant. For even if God did use sophisticated literary structure along with a great deal of anthropomorphisms and assumed ordinary providence would be understood to have been his modus operandi during the creation week, surely he knew that the way it was written could easily and quite understandably confuse his church. Why then did he write it in such a way? It strains credulity to think that God would do this in a book that he gives to his covenant children so they can know him and have eternal life. Yet, according to advocates of the Framework Hypothesis, God knowingly wrote the foundational chapter for the entire book of Genesis, which, in turn, is the foundational book of the entire Bible, in such a sophisticated manner of presentation that it would not properly be understood by his church for 2000 years.

And lest some consider this to be an abstract theological question, consider the ramifications this novel understanding of Genesis 1 has for the whole body of Christ. How do we tell Christ's little ones, who reading and meditating upon God's word understand Genesis 1 in its literal sense, that they really have not understood this portion of Scripture at all? This would not be like misunderstanding the meaning of the Song of Songs or certain difficult passages of the apostle Paul (even Peter seems to have had trouble with that). Christians, laymen and teachers alike, have difficulty with these and other texts. They seek out help in understanding them. But it would be odd to find a Christian who sought out his pastor or a seminary professor for guidance in understanding Genesis 1.[5] The meaning is clear and unambiguous to him.[6] But then the scholar comes along and says he has not really understood Genesis 1 at all. God did not create in the way the text seems to say he did. With the tools of modern scholarship we are finally in a position to understand what this passage actually means. It teaches a two-register cosmology and warns us not to follow after Baal. But, again, one thing that it definitely does not teach is that God created the universe in the space of six days.

What does this do to the Christian laymen? Necessarily his confidence in his ability to understand the Bible is undermined. Most likely his confidence in the clarity of Scripture will be undermined as well. He will likely reason that if he cannot understand the first chapter of Genesis that he has always taken to be so clear and straight forward, how can he possibly understand other passages? Perhaps he has been greatly mistaken about other texts as well. Without training in cognate studies, literary analysis, redemptive-historical hermeneutics and so on, who is he, after all, to come to a right understanding of the word of God?

Greg Bahnsen's comments are on target: "Christian scholars and especially those in seminaries can be so discouraging to the vital obedience of God's people, who are cowed into feeling 'nobody knows for sure,' even about what God clearly said."

In pondering similar ornate and complicated typologies and redemptive-historical arguments – "especially at how subtle are their alleged insights

---

[5] Note: the claim here is not that Christians never have difficulties with understanding Genesis 1 in light of the teachings of modern science. Many Christian college students, for example, wonder how to reconcile Genesis 1 with an 12 billion year-old universe. But this proves the point. The only reason they seek to reconcile the two is that they see that they are radically out of accord with one another.

[6] Saying this is not to assume the "man on the street" hermeneutic that the Majority Report implicitly accuses us of (p. 5). I am assuming here the point by point analysis and refutation of the Framework Hypothesis contained above.

or how technical one's knowledge of particular words (and word-studies) would need to be" – Bahnsen asks a reasonable question:

> I wonder whether, even if they were true, such expositions could possibly have crossed the minds or been understood by the original recipients of the Word being interpreted! Could they really have been expected to work through such a *maze* of creative connections or convoluted logic to reach a correct reading of the text and proper application of it? I really doubt it. And about that time I remember the Apostle John's thought-provoking words: "And as for you, the Anointing which you received from Him abides in you, so that you need not that anyone teach you; His Anointing teaches you concerning all things, and is true." (1 John 2:27)

Before a Presbytery can legitimize the Framework Hypothesis as a valid understanding of the Genesis 1 and 2, it must seriously consider the implications. This issue has great consequences not only for the theology and hermeneutics and the nature of our Confession, but it has will have a very real repercussions on the body of Christ.

Framework advocates have their own version of the perspicuity of Scripture as well. Indeed, the Majority Report contends forcefully that Genesis 1 is as lucid as can be:

> The picture of Genesis 1 is clear. God wakes up. He works until evening. He lies down for the night and repeats the process in the morning. *The Spirit has gone out of His way to present the work of God on the analogy of the work of man.* (Majority Report 8)

This passage is a chilling illustration of the dangerous implications of the Framework Hypothesis.

Confessional Hermeneutics

In the introductory paragraphs of section II of the Majority Report, the authors set out to define the hermeneutic of the Westminster Confession of Faith in order to help evaluate whether the Framework Hypothesis is in accord with its teaching on biblical interpretation. The following is an evaluation of their definition.

This section of the Report styles the dispute between the traditionalists (those who hold to six day creation) and the framework advocates as essentially a debate between two different approaches to Scripture: one side (the traditionalists) adheres to a literalist, "man on the street" hermeneutic while the other (the framework proponents) adheres to the Confession's hermeneutic (p. 3-4).

What then do they mean by a literalist hermeneutic and what is the hermeneutic they propose as the Confession's?

Though it is not explicitly stated, the implication one draws from the Report's discussion of the Confession's hermeneutic is that those who oppose the Framework Hypothesis adhere to a hermeneutic of mandating a literal understanding of the Bible whenever possible.[7] That is, if a biblical text can possibly be understood literally, then that is how the text should be understood. But is this really the hermeneutic of those who hold to the traditional interpretation of Genesis 1 such as Luther, Calvin, the Westminster divines, Leupold, Keil and Delitzsch, Dabney, Kuyper, Bavinck and Berkhof? Is this the hermeneutic of Wayne Grudem, Douglas Kelly, Joseph Pipa, Robert Raymond, Morton Smith, Noel Weeks, E. J. Young and the other contemporary scholars who are critical of the Framework Hypothesis? Obviously not. But this is the impression one comes away with after reading the Majority Report.[8]

After beating up on this strawman literal-where-possible, "man on the street" hermeneutic, the Majority Report proceeds to give the hermeneutic that they believe is taught in the Westminster Confession. The authors assert simply: "we use Scripture to interpret Scripture" (p. 3). They then give the following brief commentary about the implications of this hermeneutic approach:

> It is worth noting up front, then, that the Orthodox Presbyterian Church does not subscribe to a literal-where-possible-figurative-only-when-necessary hermeneutic. So if the framework interpretation fails to take the Scripture literally at a certain point, we will not be troubled by that. But if the interpretation takes one passage in a way that is undeniably contradicted by other passages, we will consider the interpretation to have

---

[7] This has echoes of Kline. The very first sentence of the précis of his "Space and Time and Cosmogony" article reads: "To rebut the literalist interpretation of the Genesis creation "week" propounded by the young-earth theorists is the central concern of this article."

[8] One also comes away with the impression that the authors of the Report believe that those who hold to the traditional view of Genesis 1 are guilty of "deny[ing] the entire system of Biblical interpretation that our Standards propose" (p. 3). Quite a serious accusation indeed.

failed. Otherwise, we must consider the interpretation to fall within the bounds of our Confession's hermeneutic. (p. 4)

Thus, according to the Majority Report, the Confession's hermeneutic is "Scripture interprets Scripture" and this implies that the church must allow any interpretation of any biblical text, figurative or literal, as acceptable unless it is "undeniably" contradicted by other passages.

This impoverished and absurd view of "our Confession's hermeneutic" is susceptible to an obvious *reductio*. According to this principle, any event or even doctrine that is mentioned only once in Scripture can be taken figuratively. Thus, one is free to interpret the floating ax-head (2 Kings 6:5), Christ's changing of the water into wine (John 2:9) Paul's raising of Eutychus (Acts 20:10) and numerous other once-mentioned miracles as figurative since there is nothing in the rest of Scripture to contradict these interpretations.[9]

Moreover, there are numerous doctrines in Scripture that are taught in only one location. For instance, the doctrine that all men by nature know the law of God is found only in Romans 2:15 (see WCF IV. 2). Notice particularly that Paul is using figurative language ("the law written on their hearts"). Are we free therefore to give this text a figurative interpretation? Perhaps Paul is using hyperbole and means only some men know God by nature. Or, worse, perhaps all of God's law is known in exhaustive detail by all men thus making the special revelation of the law superfluous. Since this is not contradicted by other portions of Scripture, anyone who held this would "fall within the bounds of our Confession's hermeneutic."

Notice also how high the Majority Report sets the bar for allowing one Scripture to bear upon another. Only if the sense of one Scripture *undeniably* contradicts the interpretation of another is the exegete compelled to change his interpretation. And apart from the fact that undeniability is somewhat subjective (what is undeniable to one may be deniable to another) it is often difficult to find a text that undeniably contradicts an obviously aberrant interpretation of another. And even if one

---

[9] One may object that such interpretations are contradicted by other Scripture since the general thrust of the recording of such events is to describe the miraculous. This may be the general thrust of Scripture, but to say it applies to every particular recording of a seemingly miraculous event is a sweeping generalization, a notorious fallacy.

is found, this gives approach gives no help with determining which interpretation has epistemological priority.

The problem is much deeper than this, however. The Majority Report's understanding of Scripture interprets Scripture, is, by itself, vacuous. In order to allow one portion of Scripture to interpret another, the interpretation of one portion must already be known. But since "the hermeneutic to which we in the OPC subscribe" does not help us out here, it would appear that the exegete is left free of biblical constraints to speculate as he pleases.

For these reasons and others, the principle of Scripture interprets Scripture obviously requires other principles of interpretation in order to function. But this is denied by the Majority Report. According to its authors, the Orthodox Presbyterian Church is confessionally obligated to allow any interpretation of any portion of Scripture that does not undeniably contradict other portions of Scripture.

Apart from the absurdities of this view, it is significant to note that the Majority Report does not even get their one hermeneutic principle right. The Confession reads: "The infallible rule of interpretation of Scripture is the Scripture itself: and therefore, when there is a question about the true and full sense of any Scripture (which is not manifold, but one), it must be searched and known by other places that speak more clearly" (WCF 1:10). From this clear and concise statement the authors of the Report infer the vague slogan, "Scripture interprets Scripture." What does this mean, though? Does this mean that the New Testament interprets the Old? Does it mean that 2 Peter is to be understood in light of Nehemiah? Does it mean that 2 Kings 18:27 (KJV) is the key that unlocks the prophecy of Ezekiel?

It is obvious that the Confession does not teach something as vague and useless as this. Indeed, what it does teach is quite plain. When the true and full sense of one portion of Scripture is difficult to ascertain, other parallel portions of Scripture that are more clear should be sought out and used to shed light on the sense of the difficult portion. There is nothing difficult to understand about this.[10]

---

[10] There is a good deal of irony in the fact that advocates of the Framework Hypothesis reverse this principle in their interpretive practice. They use a relatively unclear passage, Gen. 2:5, to interpret a perfectly clear passage, Gen. 1. There is also irony in that while the framework advocates of the Majority Report claim to follow the hermeneutic of the

Why would the authors of the Majority Report commit such a blunder? It seems their desire to legitimate the Framework Hypothesis as agreeable with our Standards has blinded them to what would otherwise be a plainly deficient presentation. For on their view, if there is no passage outside Genesis 1 that undeniably contradicts the Framework Hypothesis, then the Framework Hypothesis must be accepted by confessional Presbyterian churches. And since the authors of the Report do not in fact think a figurative approach to that text is contradicted by other portions of Scripture, the debate, at least in their minds, is effectively over.[11] Given the Majority Report's position, then, it is necessary to give a brief sketch of the actual teaching of the Confession regarding hermeneutics.

The Confession declares:

> All things in Scripture are not alike plain in themselves, nor alike clear unto all: yet those things which are necessary to be known, believed, and observed for salvation are so clearly propounded, and opened in some place of Scripture or other, that not only the learned, but the unlearned, *in a due use of the ordinary means*, may attain unto a sufficient understanding of them. (1: 7.)

This section teaches the perspicuity of Scripture. Even though there are some texts that are difficult to understand, Scripture is basically clear and plain, especially on issues pertaining to salvation. Thus not only the biblical scholar, but the uneducated (Christ's little ones) are called to read and *understand* Scripture. And the way they are to read and understand Scripture is through the diligent use of ordinary means.

What, then, are the ordinary means? Put simply, they are the means by which all competent language speakers use each time they read a newspaper, flip through a mail order catalog or read the latest work of their favorite novelist. The Bible is to be read and interpreted like any other piece of literature, in its grammatical, historical context and according to its literary genre. These basic rules of interpretation have been recognized by all of the leading Reformed theologians and exegetes. Charles Hodge is representative:

Confession, they arrive at a completely different interpretation of Gen. 1 than the Confession does.

[11] Even here they fail. There are two passages of Scripture that contradict the framework view of Gen. 1, Exod. 20:11 and Exod. 31:17.

The words of Scripture are to be taken in their plain historical sense. That is, they must be taken in the sense attached to them in the age and by the people whom they were addressed. This only assumes that the sacred writers were honest, and *meant to be understood.*[12]

These two principles, alone, however (the analogy of Scripture and the grammatical-historical method) do not exhaust the Confession's teaching on hermeneutics. The Confession teaches that the meaning of each text is singular not manifold (1:9), that the illumination of the Spirit is necessary for a saving knowledge of the truths revealed in Scripture (1:6) and that interpreters should be careful to recognize the different functions that the language of Scripture performs.

[The] Christian believes to be true whatsoever is revealed in the Word [informative function], for the authority of God Himself speaking therein; and acts differently upon that which each particular passage thereof contains; yielding obedience to the commands [directive function], trembling at the threatenings [emotive function], and embracing the promises [performative function] of God for this life, and that which is to come." (14:2)

The doctrines of the necessity (1:1), authority (1:4) and sufficiency (1:6) of Scripture, moreover, have obvious implications for biblical interpretation. The divines also take pains to give detailed rules for understanding the law of God (LC 99). Furthermore, the teaching that there is a divine and human author for all Scriptures (1:2) has many implications. Its human authorship implies that the sense of a portion of Scripture must have been known to the one who wrote it.[13] Its divine Authorship implies that it is infallible and that no Scripture can be interpreted in such a way that is inconsistent with another Scripture. And because God is the Author of all of Scripture it is to be viewed as a unified whole which has the common intent of bringing glory God himself (I. v). Finally, because there is a historical development of the covenant that centers on the Lord Jesus Christ, much of what

---

[12] Hodge, *Systematic Theology*, vol. I (Grand Rapids: Eerdmans, 1989),187 (emphasis mine).

[13] This does not mean that the author of a portion of Scripture necessarily knew the referent of what he wrote. Indeed, Peter tells us, "Concerning this salvation, the prophets, who spoke of the grace that was to come to you, searched intently and with the greatest care, trying to find out the time and circumstances to which the Spirit of Christ in them was pointing when he predicted the sufferings of Christ and the glories that would follow." (1 Pet. 1:10-11)

preceded him were types and ordinances that foresignified his perfect work of redemption (VII. 5). Thus the Confession alerts us to the use of typology in Scripture.

Quite clearly, then, the principle that Scripture interprets Scripture, even when it is properly understood, is not *the* hermeneutic of the Confession. It is only a part, albeit a crucial part, of its overall teaching on biblical interpretation. It is this full and robust hermeneutic that the Framework Hypothesis must be in accord with if it is to be deemed legitimate by our denomination.

PART IV
CONCLUDING REMARKS

Chapter 7
CONCLUSION
Kenneth L. Gentry, Jr.

The Framework Hypothesis is an influential and potent approach to the Creation account in Genesis. It possesses a certain air of sophistication that holds forth the authority of Scripture while allowing for "natural revelation" which suggest many features of evolutionary theory. Its literary approach to the interpreting Genesis 1 suggests an impressive and highly refined revelation from God to Moses some 3500 years ago. Nevertheless, appearances can be deceiving. The massive re-interpretation of the biblical record required by this literary hypothesis should give pause to any who would initially be impressed with it.

Christians committed to the traditional interpretation of Genesis will need to prepare themselves if they desire intelligently and cogently to answer the Framework objections to the historic position on Creation. Though the Framework approach has been around for over seventy-five years, it has within the past ten years begun making remarkable inroads into Reformed theology. Just as the Day Age Theory gained a certain influence among evangelicals in the early part of the Twentieth Century, it appears that the Framework Hypothesis may be doing the same in the early part of the Twenty-first Century. It will not go away by a refusal to engage it.

The authors of this work are offering this modest critique to a wider audience in the hope that it might encourage others—ministers and laymen—more vigorously to engage the debate. Initial confrontation with this sophisticated approach to the Creation account can seem overwhelming. One can easily be intimidated by the erudition so evident in the ornate structure of the system. Oftentimes Christians are cowered by the fear that they are acting as mere Bible thumpers, mindlessly promoting an out-dated party line that actually embarrasses the integrity of our holy faith. Indeed, Christian astrophysicist Hugh Ross begins his introduction to one of his books: "Nearly half the adults in the United States believe that God created the universe within the last 10,000 years. What reason do they give? 'The Bible says so.'"[14] Yet a simple survey of the list of intelligent proponents

---

[14] Hugh Ross, *Creation and Time: Biblical and Scientific Perspective on the Creation-Date Controversy* (Colorado Springs: NavPress, 1994), 7.

of the traditional approach to the Creation narrative should dispel such concerns. Furthermore, a careful analysis of the Framework Hypothesis itself—such as we have offered herein—should hearten those committed to the view that God created the world in the space of six, sequential, twenty-four hour days.

Before closing our book, we would like to suggest a brief, affordable reading list for further study. These books should be purchased, read, digested, and discussed for gaining deeper insights into both the arguments *for* the traditional view of six day creation, as well as arguments *against* literary approaches to re-interpreting the Mosaic account of creation.

Cassuto, Umberto. *A Commentary on the Book of Genesis: Part I: From Adam to Noah,* trans. Israel Abrahams. Jerusalem: Magnes, 1961.

Kelly, Douglas F. *Creation and Change.* Ross-shire, Great Britain: Mentor, 1997.

Moreland, J. P., and John Mark Reynolds, ed. *Three Views on Creation and Evolution.* Grand Rapids: Zondervan, 1999.

Pipa, Joseph A., Jr. and David W. Hall, eds, *Did God Create in Six Days?* Taylors, S. C.: Southern Presbyterian, 1999.

Weeks, Noel. *The Sufficiency of Scripture.* Edinburgh: Banner of Truth, 1988.